What Others Are Saying

"Paul described himself as a faithful Jew and a Pharisee long after his Damascus road encounter. Derek Leman has done a great service by taking this self-description seriously and reinterpreting Paul's message and impact accordingly. The book is particularly helpful in outlining the different relationship with Torah intended for Jews and Gentiles, including Jewish and Gentile Yeshua-followers. This clear and readable exposition will help Christians better understand, not only the New Testament, but also their Jewish friends and neighbors, and especially Messianic Jews."
　　　　Russ Resnik, Executive Director
　　　　Union of Messianic Jewish Congregations

"Few books are so persuasive that they change how we perceive Holy Scripture, this is one of those books. In a concise, easy to understand presentation, Derek Leman challenges many traditional misinterpretations of scripture, laying out the clear meaning of difficult passages when understood from their Historical and Jewish Cultural settings. A must read for anyone seeking a greater understanding of the teachings of our Jewish Messiah – Yeshua (Jesus)."
　　　　Cameron Bryars, Congregational Leader
　　　　Beth HaMashiach, Loganville, Georgia.

D1270468

PAUL

Didn't Eat Pork

Reappraising Paul the Pharisee

DEREK LEMAN

Mt. Olive
Press

Paul Didn't Eat Pork
Reappraising Paul the Pharisee
by Derek Leman

Published by:
Mt. Olive Press
Post Office Box 659
Stone Mountain, GA 30086
mtolivepress.com

ISBN 0-9747814-1-X Softcover

First printing 2005.

Library of Congress Control Number: 2005922274

This book is printed on archival quality paper.

Contents

About the Author

Derek Leman and his wife Linda have six children and live in Stone Mountain, Georgia. Derek is the Spiritual Leader of Hope of David Messianic Fellowship in Sandy Springs, Georgia. Derek is also a consultant to the Georgia Baptist Convention on outreach to the Jewish community.

Derek is the author of 4 books prior to *Paul Didn't Eat Pork*: *Jesus Didn't Have Blue Eyes*, the first of this series of three books, *Proverbial Wisdom and Common Sense*, a daily devotional guide to the book of Proverbs, *Walking With Yeshua*, a guide for new believers to the life that Yeshua calls us to live, and *The Y'shua Challenge Part 2*, a four-unit discussion guide for sharing the good news of Messiah with an interested Jewish friend.

Derek is available to speak to churches and other groups. He can be contacted through the website *mtolivepress.com*.

To purchase more copies of this book or any other from Mt. Olive Press, go to *mtolivepress.com* or write to:
    Mt. Olive Press
    P.O. Box 659
    Stone Mountain, GA 30086

Refer to the Quick Order Form at the back of this book.

Acknowledgements

I am so thankful for both of my families: my wife Linda and six (going on seven) children: Deborah, Nathanael, Rachel, Hannah, Josiah, and Samuel, as well as my congregational family: Hope of David Messianic Congregation.

Special thanks to my wife for urging me to finish so she can better understand Paul herself.

Thanks to my friends at Hope of David, who encourage (as well as tease me), who create an environment of study and passion for learning, and who would do anything for me and my family (as I would for theirs).

Although I don't know him, I'm grateful to Mark Nanos for commentaries that challenge the status quo and provide insight into how much more complex history and rhetoric are than we often realize.

Finally, I thank the reader for being patient when my logic doesn't seem sound and for giving new ideas the benefit of the doubt.

Preface

In the last half of the second century, an unknown writer described Paul as a short bald man with crooked legs, a hook nose, and eyebrows that met in the middle.

This fictitious image of Paul is almost certainly false. It is a symbol of the fictitious Paul of too much preaching and theologizing.

Paul the Pharisee was certainly a complex man. Of all the writers of the Bible, he is the only one singled out as difficult to read by the Bible itself. Peter said of Paul in 2 Peter 3:15-16, "Just as our beloved brother Paul also wrote to you according to the wisdom given him, as he does in all his letters when he speaks in them of these matters. *There are some things in them that are hard to understand,* which the ignorant and unstable twist to their own destruction, as they do the other Scriptures."

Reading Paul the Pharisee should be liberating. A fresh wind of holiness should blow over us as we read the disciple of the master. The way to follow Jesus the Messiah should be made plain.

It is not merely Paul's penchant for long sentences that causes us to misread him. There is also a tragic history of anti-Jewish sentiment in the church. Long before we were born, the Jewish ideas of the New Testament were virtually censored.

As with my previous book in this series, *Jesus Didn't Have Blue Eyes: Reclaiming Our Jewish Messiah,* it is my intention here only to introduce readers to a new way of looking at Paul. This book at most can be a compass guiding your journey through the epistles.

It is my hope that it will be a true compass. May it point true north, to the way of the cross. That way is foolishness to some, but the power of God to those who are being saved.

Part One
Why We Need a Reappraisal

Chapter 1
The Misunderstood Pharisee

Paul met Jesus on the road to a city in Syria called Damascus. I met him as a college student at Georgia Tech. I didn't know who Paul was, at the time, though I had heard his name.

My introduction to the faith came through the Hebrew Bible (Old Testament), the bulk of which I read before knowing the truth about Jesus. I was reading the history of a people, the Jewish people. Though not born Jewish myself, I was interested because my college fraternity was heavily Jewish.

Eventually, a friend gave me C.S. Lewis's *Mere Christianity*. I had my own "Damascus Road experience" that night after reading much of Lewis's book. I was now a Jesus-follower, but what would that mean?

My friend told me, "Now that you believe in Jesus, you have to start going to church." I wasn't happy about this. Jesus was great, I'd decided, but I had strong reservations about church.

Someone told me about a church very close to the campus of Georgia Tech. I'd never heard of it, but it was apparently large and well-known—First Baptist Church of Atlanta.

When I arrived at First Baptist, they had a class just for people like me, new believers. I was a young engineering student. I was into the college scene. I wasn't used to meeting with middle-aged people. Yet I was welcomed and strangely warmed by the music and the people sharing their stories.

They asked me for mine. When I finished telling the class, they looked at me with a blank stare. "You mean, you've never read any of the New Testament," they asked as though something were wrong with me.

"No, where does it start?" I asked. Although I had read a lot of the Hebrew Bible, I didn't understand the Bible's divisions just yet.

The next morning, I got up early and started to read Matthew. It was in Matthew 1:1 that I made my first startling discovery in my newfound faith—Jesus was Jewish (for the whole story, read my earlier book, *Jesus Didn't Have Blue Eyes*).

For the first six months or so of my journey with Jesus, I was reading the gospels. But a curious disconnect was going on between my Bible reading and my experience at church. I had read the Hebrew Bible. I was familiar with Abraham, Moses, David, and the rest. I was reading the gospels. I wanted to know more about Jesus, Peter, and the disciples. The only problem was, at church we seemed to talk only about Paul.

The predominance of Paul was very noticeable to me. After all, I barely knew who he was, so when he was mentioned I took notice. I found that the sermons at First Baptist were based on a text from Paul 90% of the time. I also noticed that Christians seemed to regard Paul as a final court of appeal for any belief.

It didn't matter if Jesus or one of the prophets had said the same thing. People had to find a verse written by Paul to prove a point beyond a shadow of a doubt. I quickly learned to follow suit.

Paul Divorced From His Roots

It seemed, as I learned from the example of my new Christian friends, that the Hebrew Bible was really just the Old Testament. It was old and out of date. The truths of the Old Testament were inspired by God, sure, but in practice they were not applicable directly.

When there was a sermon from the "Old Testament," it was usually a story which was interpreted in Christian terms. David fought Goliath as a lesson for us to have great faith. Abraham sacrificed Isaac so we would have a "type" (an allegorical picture) of the cross. Israel sinned as a moral example to Christians how not to live.

In the same way, I determined from the way Christians talked that the teaching of Jesus was also old and not directly applicable in many cases. Jesus made some strong demands for a person to be his disciple. I was assured that these were not to be taken literally. After all, they said, Paul teaches faith alone. Jesus needed to be interpreted in light of Paul.

I went along with my newly learned principles of interpreting the Bible. I know now, I was missing a lot of the richness not only of the Hebrew Bible and of Jesus' teaching, but also of Paul.

Paul did not invent Christianity. Yet for centuries many scholars have been saying that he did. These are not the kind of scholars my friends at church would have approved of. In a strange way, however, my conservative, Bible-believing church friends were agreeing with liberal scholars. They were separating Paul from Jesus. They were separating Paul from the Hebrew Bible. They were reading Paul as an innovator. They were almost saying Paul came to change what the rest of the Bible had been teaching.

False Portraits of Paul

Near the end of the second century, an unknown clergyman wrote a collection of stories about Paul. According to the church father Tertullian, this clergyman was defrocked because of the contents of his book.[1]

In *The Acts of Paul*, there is a description of the apostle:

> And he saw Paul coming, a man of small stature, with a bald head and crooked legs, in a good state of body, with eyebrows meeting and nose somewhat hooked, full of friendliness.[2]

The description of Paul as a small, hook-nosed man with a uni-brow should be taken as fiction. The account is written so long after Paul's life, there is almost no reason to take it seriously.

The false portrait of Paul in *The Acts of Paul* is only a sample of many false portraits held by his readers today. I have encountered erroneous depictions and flawed interpretations in numerous sermons and Bible discussions.

One of Paul's famous sayings is that he became as a Jew to the Jews and as one without Law to those without a Law.[3] The saying troubled me from the first time I heard it discussed, since the speaker I was listening to depicted Paul as a chameleon, eating pork with his Gentile friends and wearing a yarmulke with his Jewish associates.

Paul was no schizophrenic. He was no hypocrite. He did not fight against Peter for the truth of the gospel[4] only to live the opposite of that truth around his Jewish associates. As I will show in this book, Paul lived a lifestyle of Torah-observance and Jewish tradition. He did not fake Jewishness around his Jewish associates and enjoy suckling pig with Gentile friends.

Another faulty image of Paul is a liberator who set people free from Old Testament burdens. According to this theory, the Jews were suffering under the heavy weight of the Law. Paul saw that the cross eliminated the Law and proclaimed freedom.

As I will show in this book, Paul agreed with the whole Bible. He did not go against his master, Jesus, who said that the Law will not disappear until heaven and earth are gone.[5] Paul's writings concerning the Law, the Torah of Israel, are misunderstood. Part of the reason is that when we read Paul's letter we are reading only one side of a conversation. Another is that the church early on developed an aversion to all things Jewish and read Paul as a sort of anti-Jew.

An erroneous picture I loathe to hear is of Paul as a church man, setting Israel aside. Paul saw Israel's time as past and the church as the wave of the future. How anyone can believe this and read Romans 9-11 is beyond me, but I have certainly seen such views.

Most surprising, since Christianity is a very ethical belief system, is the warped notion of Paul as an advocate of a new ethic—do whatever you want as long as the Spirit leads. I used to be confused as a young student of the Bible when I would hear talk like this from respected teachers. I wanted to ask, "Why do we need the Bible then?" Surely Paul, who called the scriptures God-breathed, would not agree that commandments and written revelation are outdated.[6]

Benefits of Getting Paul Right

In contrast to these false portraits, there is the Paul of the New Testament. Paul the Pharisee is the right man to bring the Hebrew Bible and the Jewish Messiah to a Gentile world. If a Hellenistic Jew, a Jew whose leanings were toward Greek culture, had preached what Paul did, men might not think the message was from God. But when a Hebrew of Hebrews proclaimed a message to Gentiles without requiring them to become Jews, then that message is believable.

There can be no doubt that Paul is the master communicator of the message of Jesus. Although Paul can be misinterpreted, it remains true that his writings are among the most practical in the whole Bible. The potential for spiritual growth from reading Paul accurately is tremendous.

Paul the Pharisee remained a Pharisee. Speaking to the Sanhedrin in Acts 23:6, Paul said, "I am a Pharisee, a son of Pharisees." He never converted from Judaism to a new religion. Following Jesus is bringing true Judaism to Jews and bringing the God of Israel to Gentiles without requiring them to become Jews.

By reading Paul in his Jewish context, we will better understand his message. The pitfalls of misunderstanding are many.

Near the end of the first century a man was born who would become a bishop as well as a heretic. Marcion is famous for accepting Paul's writings as inspired and rejecting the rest of the Bible. Marcion rejected the Hebrew Bible and even came up with an idea of two gods to explain the existence of the Old Testament.[7]

Marcion thought that Paul's reference to the "God of this world" in 2 Corinthians 4:4 was to a lower god who created the physical universe.[8] The God of the New Testament was a higher God. The Old Testament God was cruel and merciless while the God of the New Testament was merciful and taught a way of love.

While almost no one would agree with Marcion today that the God revealed in Jesus is different from the God who created the world, practical Marcionism continues.

Practical Marcionism divides the Bible. The Bible has an outdated part and a grace-filled part. The ideas of Jesus and Paul are new, with almost no connection to the Hebrew Bible. Love and grace and truth are found by rejecting Jewish origins.

Imagine what it would be like to interpret Paul as a Pharisee instead of as the inventor of Christianity. Imagine if we, unlike Marcion, saw Paul as a disciple of the Jewish Messiah. Imagine if we saw Paul's writings explaining the fulfillment of the Hebrew Bible and not repudiating it.

There are some surprising truths about Paul's life and message for Christians who are not used to reading Paul as a Pharisee:

Acts 23:6	Paul remained a Pharisee for life.
Acts 20:16	Paul continued to celebrate the biblical feasts.
Acts 18:18, 21:20-26	Paul made a Nazirite vow according to Jewish Law (perhaps twice) during his career as an apostle.
Acts 21:26	Paul offered animal sacrifices after becoming a Jesus-follower. These sacrifices for a Nazirite included a sin offering.

Acts 21:24	Paul kept the Law, the Jewish Torah, including the customs.
Acts 24:14	Paul thought it important that following Jesus is in accordance with the Torah and the prophets.
Romans 7:12,16; 1 Timothy 1:8	Paul called the Torah good and holy.
1 Corinthians 9:9	Paul quoted the Torah to prove a point of practice for congregations.
Acts 16:3; Galatians 2:3	Paul had Timothy, whose mother was Jewish, circumcised but refused to do so to Titus.
Acts 15:19-21	Paul and the other apostles agreed that God did not require Gentiles to keep the whole Torah, but asked that Gentiles in the churches be respectful toward Jewish customs.

Paul's life and message were not to take Jews away from a Torah lifestyle, but to bring Gentiles near to God without making them become Jews.

Getting Paul right is not merely, however, a matter of understanding Jewish faith in Jesus. Getting Paul right matters to non-Jews as well.

Paul believed in holiness, in personal righteousness as a lifestyle. He did not see the cross as replacing the need for obedience to God. It is chiefly on this point that people misread him.

There can be no doubt that Paul preached freedom, but not freedom to sin. Paul's message was freedom from condemnation for those who believe. Paul's message was not freedom from holiness.

In many ways, getting Paul right will improve our lives as Jesus-followers.

Paul knew how to follow Jesus. He knew the balance of faith and good deeds. He knew the practical ways to enjoy God's righteousness.

If we interpret Paul correctly, we will:

- See the Bible as a whole, God's truth progressively building to the revelation of the Messiah.

- See how Paul was a student of the Hebrew Bible.

- See how Paul was a student of Jesus.

- Understand the balance of receiving salvation and living it out.

- Understand the place of Israel in God's plan and what the role of the churches should be.

- Understand the role of the Holy Spirit and the Law.

- Be able to walk in righteousness that is from God.

- Be able to explain the cross accurately to those we want to share Jesus with.

- Be able to appreciate the Jewish heritage of our faith.

Discussion Questions

• What does the attitude of most teachers and preachers seem to be regarding the authority of Paul as compared to Jesus, other apostles, or the Hebrew Bible?

• Why does the name "Old Testament" seem derogatory? What other term or terms could be used to describe it?

• Do you think Paul is the originator of significant ideas in our faith? If not the originator, do you think he received from God much original material adding to our faith and practice?

• How do you picture Paul's appearance? How did an early writer describe him? Is there much evidence for the truth of this description?

• Is it possible that many in the church have misinterpreted Paul's view of the Law? In what ways?

• How is Paul the ideal person to communicate God's acceptance of Gentiles without them becoming Jews?

• What is Marcionism and how is it similar to the way many Christians treat the Hebrew Bible?

• Of the list of Paul's Jewish lifestyle (on pages 13 and 14), which ones surprised you the most?

Chapter 2
Interlude: A Young Pharisee

His family sent him to Israel to study Torah and to become a Torah-teacher himself. He did not study with just any teacher, though, but only with the best.

This young Pharisee learned Torah from Gamaliel.[1] Gamaliel had been the personal student of Hillel, and not only the personal student, but the most renowned student.

The house of Hillel was one of two major philosophies within the sect of the Pharisees. Hillel's house was peaceable and quiet. Hillel taught that study of Torah was the way for Israel.

Israel's problem, as everyone knew, was that it was not free. Israel had not yet been restored since the days of Babylon. One tyrant nation after another had ruled and even during a time when Israel was ruled by Jews, they turned to tyrants as well.

The house of Hillel believed that the study and practice of Torah would end Israel's exile. God would deal with the Romans when the people were faithful. They needed to practice the teachings of Moses and also of the elders.

The teachings of the elders brought ceremonies from the temple into the home and into the synagogue. The family dinner table became like an altar. Everyone poured water over their hands before eating, like the priests poured water over their hands and feet before serving. Such practices would be part of the salvation of Israel.

Over time, Paul grew discontent with this teaching. There needed to be something more. He was lured by the other philosophy of the sect of Pharisees, the house of Shammai.[2]

Where Hillel was often lenient, Shammai was strict. Where Hillel invited others in, Shammai kept others out. Where Hillel was about peace, Shammai was about zeal.

The quintessential story for the house of Shammai was that of Phinehas.[3] When Israelite sinners dared to bring Moabite prostitutes into the camp, Phinehas went into a nearby tent and impaled lovers with his spear. This was zeal for the Lord.

The house of Shammai saw a need for something in addition to Torah study and tradition. They saw a need for militant action. The land would be more faithful if heretics, minim in Hebrew, were arrested or killed.

Our young Pharisee began to be very active in arresting and killing minim, especially the followers of Yeshua[4], the Nazarene.

Our young Pharisee was *Sha'ul* (shah-ool, Saul). His family was of the tribe of Benjamin. There could be no greater name in that tribe than Saul, named for the ancient king of Israel. Yet Saul's Greek name, *Paulos*, meant "small one." He certainly was not small in his zeal for the Lord.

Saul's zeal was easy to see. He had participated in stoning and imprisoning Yeshua-followers, such as that young Stephen. Saul certainly did not agree with his former mentor, Gamaliel, who said, "Keep away from these men and let them alone, for if this plan or this undertaking is of man, it will fail; but if it is of God, you will not be able to overthrow them. You might even be found opposing God!"[5]

Far from staying away from the *minim*, Saul was now on the highway to Damascus. As much as he hated submitting to the chief priests, he and his companions had no choice. So Saul had gone to them for permission.

In Damascus, Saul would arrest Yeshua-followers. They called themselves the Way. He would show them the way to imprisonment and perhaps execution. This movement of *minim* had to be stopped. Damascus was a center for them, a place where they were safe and could send emissaries out. If Saul could break their Damascus ring, then he could curtail their influence greatly. In his own way, he was helping to bring God's kingdom. By purifying the land and helping start a revival of Torah, perhaps he could be part of bringing the days of Messiah to Israel.

The chief priests had even let him bring some temple soldiers with him. For a young man, he was rising in his power and influence.

As he pondered these things, things changed suddenly. Light, then darkness. He had never seen a light so bright, brighter than the sun. Now he was blind and off his horse. He didn't remember falling, but he felt the stones and dirt and the bruises. What was happening?

The soldiers around him were startled. One called out, "Sha'ul, are you hurt?"

He heard their horses wheeling about, searching for an enemy. Why weren't they blinded like he was?

All were stilled by a voice suddenly booming from above. Of course, a light, a voice! This was the *bat kol*, the voice of God.

What would God say to him? The thought flashed through Saul's mind in an instant, "You are my servant to purify the land. You must rid the land of these *minim*." Maybe God would use him like Elijah or Jehu, who killed the followers of Baal..

He clearly heard the voice, "Sha'ul, Sha'ul, why are you persecuting me?"

This wasn't right. Persecuting? I'm helping you, Lord, he thought. Is this God's voice? That's who I expected to hear. "Who are you, Lord?" he asked weakly, feeling more than before the dirt, stones, and bruises.

"I am Yeshua, whom you are persecuting."

Yeshua? No! He was dead . . . crucified as a pretender Messiah. How could it be him? His followers were the problem. How could the dead speak?

But what were the Yeshua-followers always saying? He rose on the third day. Was it true . . . Yeshua, alive? Yes, it had to be. There was no mistaking the heavenly light and the heavenly voice.

Blind and shaking, Sha'ul felt a change from confusion to joy. If Yeshua was raised, the resurrection had begun. The dead would be raised in the days of Messiah. The very thing he longed for was coming to pass. The days of Messiah must already be here.

"Rise and enter the city, and you will be told what you are to do," Yeshua said.

Sha'ul had new orders now, not from the chief priests or his Pharisee brothers. He could see it now. His approach had been all wrong. He was persecuting those who got it, those who knew the truth.

Just as surely as he traveled to purify Israel from *minim*, Sha'ul would travel to tell the world about Yeshua.

Chapter 3
Paul Against the Torah?

I'd never heard the idea before and for a few minutes it rang true. I felt sick to my stomach, as I did during those seminary years whenever I encountered something that seemed a challenge to my faith.

I'd been reading articles about Paul, including the work of F.C. Bauer, a German theologian. According to Bauer and others after him, Paul was an innovator. Paul had his own sort of school of Christianity. Opposed to Paul was the school of James.

Paul said, "To the one who does not work but trusts him who justifies the ungodly, his faith is counted as righteousness."[1] James, on the other hand, said, "I will show you my faith by my works."[2]

Paul said, "If Abraham was justified by works, he has something to boast about."[3] James said, "Was not Abraham our father justified by works."[4]

If that wasn't a contradiction in the pages of scripture, I couldn't imagine what one would look like. I couldn't find an argument against Bauer and others who implied that James and the Jewish believers believed God accepts us for our obedience to him. Meanwhile, Paul and the Gentile believers were anti-Law (antinomian), taking Christ as abolishing the Law.

It is true that James is known to have been a Law-keeper, a reputable member of the Jewish community. Josephus says of him, "[Ananius, the High Priest] brought before them [the Sanhedrin] the brother of Jesus . . . whose name was James, and some others . . . as breakers of the Law . . . but as for those who seemed the most equitable of all the citizens, and such as were most uneasy at the breach of the Laws, they disliked what was done."[5] The New Testament also gives a portrait of a Law-keeping James.[6]

It is also true that the New Testament, in some places, could be interpreted to portray a division between James and the Jerusalem congregation, on the one hand, and Paul and the Gentile congregations on the other. Paul said that "certain men came from James"[7] who directly or indirectly influenced Peter to break table-fellowship with Gentiles.

Could F.C. Bauer and other interpreters be right? Has the community of Jesus-followers been divided into camps from the beginning? Is the New Testament a contradictory document?

Christian Interpreters of Paul as Anti-Torah

Plenty of Christian interpreters through the years have seen Paul as opposed to either part or all of the Torah (the commandments of Moses). In the statements listed below, I have tried to be sure I am not quoting any writer out of context. The writers quoted are all respected commentators or pastors.

Writer	Statement
Leon Morris	"Paul saw that to add obedience to the ritual commands of the Old Testament was to make a mockery of the Christian teaching . . ."[8]
Leon Morris	"The multitude of regulations (the Jews found 613 commandments in the Law, the books Genesis to Deuteronomy) was such that even to remember them all was a burden, and to keep them all bordered on the impossible."[9]
Scott McKnight	"So, what is going on in Galatians is that the Judaizers did not change with the times; they failed to see that when Christ came, the era of the Law ended."[10]
James Montgomery Boice	". . . the reign of Law has ended for those believers who now through the coming of Jesus have become mature sons and daughters of God."[11]
John Stott	"Jesus abolished both the regulations of the ceremonial Law and the condemnation of the moral Law."[12]

To be sure, there are many statements in Paul that speak of something that has changed regarding the Law. Below is a partial list of verses that could be interpreted to mean that Paul no longer felt the commandments of Moses had any authority:

Rom. 3:21	The righteousness of God has been manifested apart from the Law, although the Law and the Prophets bear witness to it.
Rom. 6:14	For sin will have no dominion over you, since you are not under Law but under grace.
Rom. 7:4	Likewise, my brothers, you also have died to the Law through the body of Christ
Rom. 7:6	But now we are released from the Law, having died to that which held us captive
Rom. 8:2	For the Law of the Spirit of life has set you free in Christ Jesus from the Law of sin and death.
Rom. 10:4	For Christ is the end of the Law for righteousness to everyone who believes.
1 Cor. 9:20	To those under the Law I became as one under the Law (though not being myself under the Law) that I might win those under the Law.
Gal. 3:13	Christ redeemed us from the curse of the Law by becoming a curse for us.
Gal. 4:24-25	So then, the Law was our guardian until Christ came, in order that we might be justified by faith. But now that faith has come, we are no longer under a guardian.
Gal. 5:18	But if you are led by the Spirit, you are not under the Law.
Eph. 2:15	abolishing the Law of commandments and ordinances, that he might create in himself one new man in place of the two.

Yet there are also numerous statements in Paul which uphold the Law or use the Law to back up a commandment from Paul:

Rom. 2:13	For it is not the hearers of the Law who are righteous before God, but the doers of the Law who will be justified.
Rom. 3:31	Do we then overthrow the Law by this faith? By no means! On the contrary, we uphold the Law.
Rom. 7:7	What then shall we say? That the Law is sin? By no means!
Rom. 7:12	So the Law is holy, and the commandment is holy and righteous and good.
Rom. 7:14	For we know that the Law is spiritual, but I am of the flesh, sold under sin.
Rom. 7:22	For I delight in the Law of God, in my inner being.
Rom. 7:25	So then, I myself serve the Law of God with my mind, but with my flesh I serve the Law of sin.
Rom. 8:4	in order that the righteous requirement of the Law might be fulfilled in us, who walk not according to the flesh but according to the Spirit.
Rom. 8:7	For the mind that is set on the flesh is hostile to God, for it does not submit to God's Law.
1 Cor. 9:8-9	Does not the Law say the same? For it is written in the Law of Moses, "You shall not muzzle an ox when it treads out the grain."
1 Cor. 14:34	For they are not permitted to speak, but should be in submission, as the Law also says.
Gal. 3:21	Is the Law then contrary to the promises of God? Certainly not! For if a Law had been given that could give life, then righteousness would indeed be by the Law.
1 Tim. 1:8	Now we know that the Law is good, if one uses it Lawfully.

These references raise many questions about what Paul means by phrases like "under the Law" and "released from the Law" and "end of the Law" as well as "serve the Law" and "uphold the Law."

Balancing Paul the Pharisee and the Emissary to the Gentiles

Part of the interpreter's task in understanding Paul is to balance varying statements and actions of Paul to understand who he really was and what he really stood for. Some are willing to say that Paul was contradictory, keeping the Law and commandments in Acts and then teaching against them later. Some would say that Paul expected Jews to keep all the Law's commandments and taught that Gentiles did not need to keep all of them. Some would say that Paul didn't want anyone to feel the need to obey the commandments of the Law or, the reverse, he demanded that everyone keep it.

The first part of the picture of Paul needs to come from the book of Acts, where we see Paul's behavior, as well as biographical notes in his epistles. From the book of Acts we observe that Paul offered sacrifices at the temple and kept not only the Law of Moses, but also the traditions and customs.13 From the book of Acts, we observe that Paul had Timothy circumcised.14 From 1 Corinthians, we observe that Paul could prove a point of congregational practice from the Law.15 Paul did not seem anti-Torah in his actions.

The second part of the picture is Paul's complex series of teaching about the Law. Behind each teaching were ideas that threatened to throw the young congregations off track. We might think that someone who offered sacrifices and even kept the traditions of the elders (which go beyond the requirements of the Law), and yet said "Christ is the end of the Law"[16] is being contradictory. Yet Paul's statement that Christ is the end of the Law is one of many misunderstood phrases in the apostle's writing.

Christ, The End of the Law

In its context, Paul's statement about Christ being the end of the Law is part of a discussion about those in Israel who missed it—missed God's free offer of righteousness. Paul testified to the zeal his Jewish brothers had for God, but noted that they sought "to establish their own" righteousness.[16] The issue is not Law versus Lawlessness, but self-righteousness versus God-righteousness.

The context of Romans 10:4, then, is simple. Paul is going to answer how Messiah relates to righteousness. Paul's Jewish brothers and sisters were seeking righteousness on their own based on their interpretation of the Torah. Paul's answer was to say, "Christ is the end of the Law [Torah] for righteousness to everyone who believes."

The common interpretation is that he meant, "Christ's coming means the completion of the Law which is now obsolete." There are several reasons why this interpretation cannot be correct:

1. This is the wrong definition of the word translated "end."

2. Paul would be making the wrong argument: implying that they could find their own righteousness if they would just look elsewhere besides the Torah.

With regard to the word "end," we sometimes use it in English the same way Paul used the Greek word telos. When we say, "To what end are you doing this?" or "the end doesn't justify the means," we are using the word end in the sense of "goal."

Telos almost always means goal or the logical end of a progression rather than the demise of something. For example, Matthew 10:22 says, "But the one who endures to the end will be saved." The end here is the goal: the one who reaches the finish line with faith intact will be saved.

At times, telos does refer to end as in the demise of something or someone. In Mark 3:26, Jesus said that if Satan opposes himself "he cannot stand, but is coming to an end." In this case end means undesirable end or destruction.

Suppose Paul meant *telos* in this sense in Romans 10:4 rather than in the sense of goal or purpose. His argument would look like this:

1. My Jewish brothers are lost because they seek self-righteousness instead of God-righteousness.

2. The Torah is about self-righteousness.

3. Christ came to end the Torah and thus self-righteousness.

This argument would be nonsensical for two reasons. First, the Torah is not about self-righteousness, but obedience and love for God. Second, Paul did not say the Torah was the problem, but that self-righteousness was the problem.

Paul's argument could be better understood this way:

1. My Jewish brothers interpret the Torah as a system of self-righteousness.[17]

2. True righteousness is a gift from God that comes through Jesus.

3. My Jewish brothers should have seen this, since Jesus is the goal to which the Torah was pointing.

This argument makes much more sense. The middle term of this argument has been the subject of much of the early part of the book of Romans. Christ being the goal to which the Law pointed makes a lot more sense as an answer to Paul's Jewish brothers than saying Christ brought the demise of the Law.

What Are the "Anti-Law" Texts About?

Paul the Pharisee said "you also have died to the Law."[18] Paul who observed the Law of Moses and the Jewish customs spoke of "not being myself under the Law."[19] Paul who offered sacrifices at the temple and took a Nazirite vow according to the Law of Moses said, "Christ redeemed us from the curse of the Law."[20]

Paul who himself loved the Torah and found it as a book pointing to Jesus did not disagree with Jesus who said that no iota or dot will pass from the Torah. Paul knew that Jesus is the answer for Israel. Israel cannot save itself from exile by keeping the Torah. For Paul, the Torah is God's instruction book and his covenant with his people Israel.

The statements in Paul that seem anti-Law are not. The statements can be divided into several categories:

1. Those which speak of our being free from the condemnation and curses of the Law: Rom. 6:14, 7:4, 7:6, 8:2; Gal. 3:13, 4:24-25, 5:18.

2. Those which speak of salvation being separate from Law-keeping and/or Jewishness: Rom. 3:21.

3. Those which speak of Messiah showing the Law's true purpose: Rom. 10:4.

4. Those which differentiate Paul from Jews who felt their acceptance by God was through Law-keeping and/or Jewishness: 1 Cor. 9:20.

5. Those which express that any and all division between Jews and Gentiles has been removed in the body of Messiah: Eph. 2:15.

What Paul does not say, and if he did he would be in contradiction to Jesus in Matthew 5:17, is that the Law is no longer God's standard. Paul does not say that God's commandments are not applicable to believers today.

We sense this ourselves, for even when speaking of being free from the Law, we do not think this means a license to sin. The Law is the Torah, God's commandments through Moses. The Law is spiritual, holy, and good.

The supposedly anti-Torah Paul disappears upon close examination. There was no dispute between Paul and James. There were not two factions in the early congregations on different sides of the Law question.

Meanwhile, we need a reappraisal of Paul because Paul did not say what many have preached for years that he said. We need a reappraisal of Paul because he has been read as one superseding all previous scripture. We need a reappraisal of Paul because understanding Paul in light of the rest of the Bible will only help us to understand this faithful apostle better.

Discussion Questions

• What was F.C. Bauer's theory about Paul in relation to James and Peter?

• What does Josephus record about James?

• What do many commentators say about Paul and the Law?

• What kinds of phrases in Paul's writings seem to be anti-Law?

• What phrases in Paul's writings are pro-Law?

• What is the meaning of Romans 10:4?

• How can Paul's apparent anti-Law statements be understood?

Part Two

Examining Paul's Life
and Thought

Chapter 4
Acts and Paul

On the road to Syria to arrest followers of Yeshua the Nazarene, Paul discovered that the days of Messiah had come. Having thought one way most of his life, Paul's orientation changed dramatically in one conclusive vision.

Paul's readers can undergo a similar reorientation when considering the Paul of Acts. Much of popular opinion about Paul is formed from a cursory reading of his letters. Few people take the Paul of Acts seriously or even know much about him. Those who do might have a dramatic change of belief nearly comparable to Paul's vision of Jesus. Paul kept the Law all his life and expected that other Jews would do the same.

Paul and his Nazirite Vow

"Where does it say that Paul offered sacrifices at the temple?" the young woman challenged me. The group of college students were incredulous. Paul turned his back on Judaism. Everyone knows that.

I showed them Acts 21:26, which shows Paul participating in a Nazirite vow. The text says, "he purified himself along with them."

"Well, that doesn't say he offered sacrifices?" the young woman retorted.

The encounter was a perfect illustration of how the Bible is misunderstood. The young woman was unaware of the meaning and method of the sacrifices and the Nazirite vow. She was able to remain in the dark about a potentially revealing insight into Paul precisely because Jewish elements in the story remained to her a closed book.

In her mind, purification might have been merely a matter of prayer, not bloody sacrifice in an outdated temple complex. The thought of Paul, a Christian, offering an animal sacrifice was never entertained as a possibility in her reading of the story.

The whole story of Paul's participation in the Nazirite vow is not told. The story is more complex than a one-verse summary can make clear. The basic facts would seem to be: Paul paid for the sacrifices for himself and four men who were under a vow. The first purification took place at the beginning of a seven day period and there was to be a final purification at the end of seven days. The final purification did not take place because Paul was seized by a mob.[1]

Some detective work is necessary to reconstruct the story of Paul's Nazirite vow. First, the mention of seven days suggests something out of the ordinary. Nazirite vows ordinarily lasted thirty days or multiples thereof according to the Mishnah.[2] The mention of a seven-day period suggests that one or all of the men had become ritually defiled during an existing Nazirite vow which was already under way. Numbers 6:9-11 legislates that those who come in contact with a corpse during their vow period must shave the head on the first and seventh day and make offerings on the eighth day.

Paul may have still been under a Nazirite vow from his time in Cenchreae several years earlier[3] or was simply purifying himself along with the men who needed to restart their Nazirite vow.

The one odd note in the Acts story is that Paul and the other men purified themselves at the beginning of the seven days and were waiting to finish their purification at the end. There are two possibilities: the purification referred to on the first day may have simply been shaving of the hair and appearing before the priest. Or perhaps in Paul's day there was an additional sacrifice made at the beginning of the seven days.[4]

Whatever the case may be, Paul either offered animal sacrifices when he purified himself or intended to offer them at the end of the seven day period. What kind of sacrifices would he offer?

Numbers 6:14-15 requires five offerings of the Nazirite: a burnt offering, sin offering, peace offering, grain offering, and drink offering. The required animals for the five men in Paul's group would include: five male lambs, five ewe lambs, five rams, and the accompanying offerings of grain, wine, and olive oil. The cost of such an offering is staggering, which is why the four men needed a sponsor to afford the offerings.

Yet the young woman's doubts about Paul offering sacrifices reflects legitimate concerns a modern Jesus-follower might have reading this story. Would Paul need animal sacrifices, especially a sin offering, when he had put his faith already in the offering of Messiah?

Again, though the question is important, it again illustrates the popular misreading of Paul. By not understanding the true purpose of the animal sacrifices, many Jesus-followers assume that the cross eliminated the need for them. Few Christians read Leviticus or read it thoughtfully.

The animal sacrifices were never miniature versions of the cross, bringing forgiveness to the offerer.[5] The animal sacrifices purified the tabernacle (or temple) from the sin stains of the people living in the land. The regular offering of sacrifices kept the land ritually pure so the holy God could continue to dwell there.[6] Thus, not only do animal sacrifices have a different purpose than the cross, but they will be resumed in the Messianic Age when the temple is rebuilt and Jesus rules the earth from Jerusalem for 1,000 years.[7]

Those who want to understand Paul's message, and his view of the Torah in particular, need to understand the Paul of Acts, the man who offered animals on the altar at the temple in Jerusalem.

Paul Zealous for the Torah and Traditions

"Paul found freedom from the Law of Moses and the traditions of the Jews when he came to faith in Jesus," one can imagine almost any Bible teacher proclaiming. There is just enough truth in the words to be persuasive for those who will not look further into Paul's life and teaching.

Yes, Paul was free from the Law and said so himself in 1 Corinthians 9:20 and other verses. Yet what Paul was free from was not the obligation to keep the Law, whose commandments are holy and good, but from the condemnation of the Law.

If anyone says that Paul changed his lifestyle and quit obeying the Law or taught other Jews to do so, they are speaking in ignorance of the Paul of Acts. James, brother of Jesus, put it to Paul this way, "[The Jewish believers in Jesus here in Judea] have been told about you that you teach all the Jews who are among the Gentiles to forsake Moses, telling them not to circumcise their children or walk according to our customs."[8]

The concern raised about Paul was three-fold:

1. Was Paul teaching Jews to forsake Torah?

2. Was Paul teaching Jews not to circumcise?

3. Was Paul teaching Jews to abandon Jewish customs added to the Laws of Torah?

James clearly knew the charges to be false and did not even entertain them as true. He was certain that, contrary to popular opinion about Paul in our time, the apostle would never say to Jews: forsake the Torah of Moses, forsake circumcision, and quit keeping Jewish customs which are added to the Torah.

Knowing this fact leads us to a vital principle in interpreting Paul's letters: Paul fully expected Jews to obey the commandments of the Torah and maintain even the traditions of the Jewish people (when they didn't violate the spirit of Torah).

Notice that James did not say, "They have been told that you are teaching Gentiles not to circumcise or obey Moses." The Gentiles are a separate issue entirely and that became the subject of the Jerusalem Council.

Acts 15 and the Jerusalem Council

"2,000 years ago, people didn't ask how you could be Jewish and believe in Jesus? Instead they thought, 'Gentiles for Jesus? That's crazy, like a vegetarian for beef!'" he said to the Sunday morning audience in a Baptist church.[9] Truly he was right, for the Jerusalem Council of Acts 15 illustrates how modern thinking about Jews, Gentiles, and Messiah has reversed over time.

The Jerusalem Council decided that Gentiles should not be troubled to keep certain commandments of Moses.[10] Especially it decided that Gentiles need not be circumcised and convert to Jewishness[11] in order to be saved.

Imagine what the world would look like today had it not been for the Jerusalem Council. Gentiles would have had to convert and be circumcised (ouch!) in order to become followers of Jesus. In addition to Jesus, people would have had to take on the yoke of a new national identity. It would have been Messiah plus conversion instead of just Messiah. When telling your friends about Jesus, you would have to convince them to change their whole culture.

The issue before the Council was simple: some in the new Jesus-movement were saying that "unless you are circumcised according to the custom of Moses, you cannot be saved."[12] In Jerusalem, some Pharisees who believed in Jesus added another clause: "and to order them to keep the Law of Moses."[13]

As an aside, we should note that being a Pharisee did not put one at odds with faith in Jesus. Paul remained a Pharisee all his days.[14] These Pharisee followers of Jesus may have been wrong about Gentiles and the

Law, but there is no evidence that they later refused to accept the decree of the apostles at the Council. Also, it is not true to think that no influential Jews decided to follow Jesus. Not only were some Pharisees believers, but also some of the priests.[15]

Regarding the issue of Gentiles following Jesus, Paul and Barnabas opposed the Gentile-conversion model. Paul had been fighting this battle for a long time. Galatians was probably written prior to the Jerusalem Council. Otherwise, Paul would have referred to it when arguing with the Jewish proselytizers of Galatians. And in Galatians, the entire issue is whether Gentiles must be converted in order to be saved.

Peter also opposed the Gentile-conversion model. He reminded the Council of the story of Cornelius and the Gentiles who received the Holy Spirit by faith. As Peter observed, God "made no distinction between us and them."[16]

Finally, James spoke. Already Paul, Barnabas, and Peter had weighed in on this important issue. Would James, the brother of Jesus and most respected elder of the congregation (along with Peter) agree with these heavyweights?

James' answer is somewhat complex. First, he notes that God has "taken from them [the Gentiles] a people for his name."[17] His statement is worded precisely. He did not say, "God has accepted Gentiles as Jews." Rather, God has called Gentiles to himself without conversion.

Then James quotes Amos 9:11-12, a prophecy remarkable for one particular phrase, "Gentiles who are called by my name." In the past, there have been people who joined Israel and came to Israel's God, such as Ruth. Yet they did not remain Gentiles, but joined Israel. Numerous prophecies in the Hebrew Bible speak of times when many Gentiles will join with Israel.[18] Amos speaks of an even greater phenomenon: Gentiles who remain Gentiles while becoming followers of Israel's God.[19]

James then renders his judgment: "we should not trouble those of the Gentiles who turn to God,"[20] yet we must ask them to abstain from four things. The four abstentions are: meat sacrificed to idols, strangled meat, blood, and sexual immorality.

Not troubling the Gentiles was James' way of saying, "Let's not make them live as Jews." While some held that only conversion and joining Israel could save Gentiles on the day of God's judgment, James knew otherwise. And if Gentiles converted, they would then be under obligation as Jewish proselytes to observe all the Law of Moses—including parts only required of Jews.

Instead of requiring Gentiles to wear fringes on the garments, maintain Jewish food Laws, and observe Jewish holy days and temple worship, James commanded four prohibitions. Their meaning is a matter of debate.

Some see these as a form of the Noahide Laws. The Noahide Laws are based in Genesis 9, where God commanded all the people (not Jews, but Gentiles) to abstain from eating blood and from murder. From this chapter, the rabbis derived seven Laws for mankind, which they said were God's only requirement for non-Jews. However, James' list looks quite different from the Noahide Laws.

Another view is that James was addressing the problems of table fellowship between Jews and Gentiles eating together. Jews and Gentiles would eat better if the Gentiles abstained from blood, idol-meat, strangled meat, and sexual immorality. This view is also impossible for two reasons: sexual immorality has nothing to do with table fellowship and unclean meats (such as pork) would be just as much a problem as strangled meat.

Tim Hegg offers a better interpretation in his book, *The Letter Writer: Paul's Background and Torah Perspective*. He notes that the four items mentioned best fit the description of practices in the pagan temples.[21] Pagan temples were the heart of life in most Roman towns. They were meat markets where portions of sacrifices (those that were not burned for the gods) were sold. Sexual immorality was also common, as some temples involved fertility cults and temple prostitution. Meat was sometimes strangled instead of being killed by slaughtering and draining blood. Hegg even provides evidence that drinking blood sometimes occurred amongst the priests.

Why did James address these issues? The answer is simple: the biggest change Gentiles coming into the Jesus movement would experience was leaving the pagan temples. For the apostles' not to require this would be tantamount to allowing idolatry amongst the congregation. Even Naaman the Syrian understood this way back in the days of Elisha. He asked the prophet's (and God's) forgiveness in advance for the fact that he would have to accompany his king into the temple of his nation's god.[22]

The effect of the Jerusalem Council would change the world. Gentiles could come to Israel's God and Israel's Messiah without having to join Israel as a people.[23] Yet the Gentiles would need to recognize some immediate changes in the life and practice if they would worship in the same congregation with Jewish followers of Jesus.

Gentiles and the Torah

The apostles specifically decided at the Jerusalem Council not to require Gentiles to be circumcised or obey the Torah of Moses as a whole. Yet a great deal of qualification is required here.

Namely, the apostles did not mean, as many modern readers assume, that the Law of Moses has no application to Gentiles. Those at the Jerusalem Council were not like modern Dispensationalist theologians who say that God's ways with man change in different eras. The Law is the old era and only commandments found in the New Testament continue to apply. Nor were the apostles modern Reformed theologians who divide the Law into categories: moral, ceremonial, and civil. Under this perspective, it is commonly assumed that only the so-called moral Laws of the Torah have continuing validity.[24] Neither of these views best synthesizes the evidence of the whole of scripture.

The apostles, as we know from the later dialogue between James and Paul in Acts 21, assumed everyone knew that Jews must continue to keep the Torah even as followers of Jesus. Yet Gentiles have a different relationship to the Torah than Jews.

God has never required that non-Israelites keep certain Laws which were given to separate Israel from the nations. God required Israel to circumcise their males on the eighth day to set Israelites apart as a covenant people. God required Israelites to observe the seventh-day Sabbath as a sign between him and Israel forever.[25] God required Israelites to wear fringes on their garments as markers of their identity.[26] God required Israelites to make a pilgrimage three times a year to Jerusalem,[27] but certainly didn't expect Gentiles to do so. God required Israel to restrict its diet of meat to certain species and to avoid accidentally killed animals.[28] God did not forbid, but allowed non-slaughtered meat to be sold to Gentiles.[29]

This is what James meant by Gentiles not being troubled about the Torah. He did not mean that Gentiles should feel free to violate any and all commandments of God in the books of Moses. Rather, Gentiles do not have to become Jews. Therefore their relationship to the Torah remains a Gentile relationship. The commandments of Torah do still apply to Gentiles, unless a commandment is limited in application to Israel.

The Jerusalem Council was not about Lawlessness, but a proper understanding of Gentiles serving God as Gentiles. This misunderstanding has cost many churches a valuable part of the Bible. Many Christians feel the books of Moses are in the Bible, but not relevant for Gentiles. The Torah is for everyone with only a few commands limited to Israel.

Yet some have misunderstood James's argument in a different direction. Maybe he wasn't saying Gentiles don't need to be troubled with circumcision and other Jewish-specific commands. Maybe he meant, "We don't need to bother the Gentiles now about keeping these commands, because they will learn the Torah later in synagogue and then start keeping them."

Moses is Taught in the Synagogues

"Gentiles have the same relationship to Torah as Jews," he said. "James said that Moses was taught in the synagogues, meaning that the Gentiles would learn the Torah later as they attended synagogue."

I found the teaching very persuasive the first few times I heard it. Perhaps that is what James meant: only bother the Gentiles now with four issues and they'll learn the rest later in synagogue.

James said, "For from ancient generations Moses has had in every city those who proclaim him, for he is read every Sabbath in the synagogues."[30] I looked in a well-written commentary by a respected scholar and found this explanation of James's comment: "James's concluding statement is puzzling. It may be regarded as saying that since there are Jews everywhere who regularly hear the Law of Moses being read in the synagogues, Gentile Christians ought to respect their scruples."[31] I didn't find this answer very convincing.

Later, I read an article by a Messianic Jewish leader who I felt truly captured the meaning of the statement.[32] In context, James has just shown that God's plan was to call Gentiles to himself as Gentiles, without making them become Jews. He is celebrating the movement of Gentiles turning to God and rejecting the call to convert them. In that vein, James notes that Moses has for generations (past) been preached in synagogues. The past part is very important.

His point is not that Gentiles can learn the Torah in the future by attending synagogue. That would be unlikely anyway. In Rome, Jews were being forced out of the synagogue for believing in Jesus.[33] It is very unlikely that Gentile Jesus-followers were going to be able to stay in them or that James would think this possible. His point is that Gentiles have been hearing Moses read in synagogues for generations and that never started this powerful movement of God that the apostles were now seeing amongst the Gentiles.

The God-fearers were Gentiles who attended synagogue to listen and learn without becoming proselytes. They had been doing so for generations and yet no mass-movement of Gentiles was turning to Israel's God.

James understood that God was doing something more powerful and amazing than converting Gentiles. God was accepting Gentiles as Gentiles. The power of God was already starting to change the Roman empire.

Paul's Jewish Observance in Acts

Understanding the relationship of Jews and Gentiles to the Torah clears up much confusion in interpreting Paul. One could easily think that the Paul of Acts must be a different person than the Paul of the letters. The Paul of Acts is a Torah-observant Jew. The Paul of the letters refuses to allow Gentiles to be made to follow the whole Torah.

Yet for all of Paul's statements about not being under the Law, there exists alongside them the record of Paul in the book of Acts.

Paul attended synagogue when he entered a town without a congregation of Jesus-followers.[34] Paul observed the Sabbath.[35] Paul kept Israel's festivals.[36] Paul remained a Pharisee.[37] Paul was careful to observe the Laws of the Torah as well as the customs of the Jewish people.[38]

Anyone reading Paul's letters must understand this or a dangerous misinterpretation will result. That dangerous misinterpretation shows up every time someone challenges those of us in Messianic Judaism by saying, "Hey, we're not under the Law. Why are you doing these things?"

A dangerous misinterpretation occurs in the other direction when critics say of the church, "They are pagan. They don't keep the Biblical holidays. They violate the Sabbath. They eat unclean meat."

Truly these issues are not minor. They are in many cases the very reason why Paul wrote his letters.

Discussion Questions

- How does lack of knowledge of the Torah keep people from understanding verses like Acts 21:26?

- What happens during a Nazirite vow?

- What was the true purpose of animal sacrifices?

- What had some in Jerusalem heard about Paul?

- What is the truth about Paul, the Law, and Jewish customs?

- What scripture did James use to prove Gentile inclusion? How did he interpret the scripture?

- What are the Noahide Laws?

- What better explains the four prohibitions of James for Gentiles to observe?

- What are some Torah commandments not required of Gentiles?

- What are two possible interpretations of the statement that "Moses has had in every city those who proclaim him"?

- What is the problem with assuming that Gentile followers of Jesus would be able to attend synagogue in their towns?

Chapter 5
Close-Up — Paul Preaching to Jews and God-Fearers

Paul had been a follower of Jesus for 13 years. His own congregation in Antioch of Syria sent him out with Barnabas to be an emissary for the good news, especially to the Gentiles.

Before turning to Jesus, Paul had accepted the view of the Sanhedrin regarding him: Yeshua the Nazarene was dead and his memory should be erased. Yet on the way to erase more followers of this Yeshua, Paul saw a heavenly light, which blinded him, and heard a voice.

He had expected the voice to commission him as God's instrument to rid the world of the Nazarenes. Instead, the voice was Yeshua, Jesus, the one Paul thought dead. Now Paul knew—Jesus was alive. He knew the resurrection had already begun. He knew God's kingdom had already started even though it was not yet complete.

Now, thirteen years later, commissioned by his brothers and sisters in Syrian Antioch, Paul was on a journey. After various adventures on the island of Cyprus, they had arrived in Pisidian Antioch—in Asia Minor (modern day Turkey) just south of Galatia.

Paul's Audience

Paul's first duty in Pisidian Antioch was to attend synagogue on the Sabbath.[1] After thirteen years of following Jesus, Paul was not separated from the synagogue. There were no house-congregations started yet in Pisidian Antioch, so Paul went to the place of worship—the synagogue. Much like the house congregations of Jesus-followers, the synagogues in many Roman towns were in houses.[2]

In the synagogue service of Paul's day, there were liturgical prayers and psalms as well as readings from the Torah (books of Moses) and the prophets. The modern synagogue service is similar though much longer, with prayers added through the centuries.

After the reading from the Torah and prophets, the synagogue leader (called the president today and the nasi or ruler in Paul's day) asked Paul to give a message. Why would he do this?

Perhaps Paul had introduced himself: Saul, student of Rabban Gamaliel the Elder. Perhaps Paul didn't need to introduce himself. He may have been known by sight as a former leader in Pharisaism. There is also another intriguing possibility: Paul may have worn distinctive dress that marked him as a Pharisee, or even a high-ranking Pharisee.

Starting his message, Paul addressed his hearers. He called them "Men of Israel and you who fear God."[3] He might have meant that the men of Israel in the synagogue were also men who fear God. Yet this is not likely, because we know that there were Gentiles who attended the synagogue who were called God-fearers.

Luke differentiated between three groups in Acts: Jews, proselytes to Judaism[4], and God-fearing Gentiles.[5] These God-fearers were Gentiles who attended synagogue without becoming proselytes, which would involve circumcision (painful to say the least).

Consider the significance of the scene: Paul, thirteen years a Jesus-follower, is quite comfortable in the synagogue preaching to Jews and God-fearers in the regular message time of the synagogue service. Is this the picture of Paul you've held all the years you've known him?

Paul's Message

More surprising than Paul's synagogue attendance and his audience was his message. In Acts 13:17-41, Paul preached a powerful message about the cross in completely Jewish terms:

Vss. 17-22	God's mighty acts for Israel leading up to the kings: Saul and David.
Vs. 23	From David's line God has brought to us a Savior.
Vss. 24-25	John the Baptizer confirmed that such a Savior would come.[6]

Vss. 26-28	Not believing the words of the prophets, the Sanhedrin ironically fulfilled the prophets by having Yeshua killed.
Vss. 29-37	Yeshua the Nazarene was raised from the dead according to the prophets and psalms and many witnesses.
Vs. 38	Forgiveness of sins comes from Yeshua.
Vs.39	Everything Moses could not free us from, this Yeshua has freed us from.
Vss. 40-41	Don't let God's startling solution pass you by merely because this is not how you thought God would do it.

Could there be a more Jewish message than the one Paul preached in that synagogue? From David's line a Savior has come. The Sanhedrin fulfilled the prophets by doubting their foretelling of just such a Savior. He was raised from the dead just as the prophets and psalms said. He has set us free in a way that the Torah never was intended to set us free.

If Paul had intended to make a break with Judaism and call his Jewish brothers to a new religion, wouldn't his message have been different?

1. God has brought a new and better way.

2. The Torah of Moses is God's old way replaced by the new way of Yeshua.

3. God is calling for you to come out of the synagogue and leave the old, unclean way.

4. God is calling you to leave behind your traditions, for they only separate and divide humankind.

5. God is calling you to come into the new way, into our congregation, in which Jewish traditions and Laws of Moses are no longer practiced.

I have heard statements like those above in plenty of Christian sermons. The Law of Moses was a burden. The traditions of the Jews made the burden even worse. Jesus came to set us free from the burdens of those commandments and bring us something new and better. The Law is obsolete now that the cross has come.

I have even heard of Jewish followers of Jesus being told to quit being Jewish: "How about a ham sandwich, my Jewish sister? So, your family maintained their Jewish identity for 3,500 years. They made it through wars, famines, and the destruction of Jerusalem twice. They made it through the Crusades, Inquisition, Pogroms, Ghettos, and even the Holocaust, and still remained Jewish in identity, tied to the people of Israel and the tradition of the rabbis. Aren't you glad you are giving all that up? In Messiah there is neither Jew nor Gentile, so why must you insist on acting Jewish? Be more Gentile, that's what Jesus wants!"

Yet, even down to the details of his message, Paul proclaimed a Jewish Messiah to an audience of Jews and Gentile God-fearers. Far from telling them to leave their synagogue, he called on them to see the goal of their Judaism as Jesus.

The Cross was a Tree

One Jewish element that may escape the notice of many readers is Paul's use of the word tree instead of cross. There is no doubt historically that Jesus died on a cross. Simon the Cyrene carried his cross-beam.[7] That many thousands of Jews died on Roman crosses is a matter of ordinary history.

Paul was not denying that Jesus was killed on a cross. He himself used the word cross many times.[8] Rather, Paul was making a point to his Jewish hearers, one they would never forget. Nor was he stretching the truth, since a cross is clearly made from a tree. A person who is hanged on a cross with nails, rope, and agony can also be said to be hanged on a tree.

What point did Paul make by using the word tree instead of cross? He no doubt made his audience think of the words of Deuteronomy 21:23, "His body shall not remain all night on the tree, but you shall bury him the same day, for a hanged man is cursed by God."

In the Torah, God instructed his people to bury dead bodies of executed criminals before sundown. The one hanged on a tree is cursed by God. Jesus was hanged on a tree. Jesus was cursed by God.

How was Jesus cursed by God? The curses of the Torah are harsh.

Leviticus speaks of "wasting disease and fever that consumes the eyes" and "heart ache."[9] It goes on to describe God setting his face against the ones cursed so that they are struck down before their enemies.[10] Deuteronomy says, "You shall grope at noonday, as the blind grope in darkness, and you shall not prosper in your ways."[11]

Paul was intimating to his audience what he said elsewhere, "Christ redeemed us from the curse of the Law by becoming a curse for us—for it is written, 'Cursed is everyone who is hanged on a tree.'"[12]

On the tree set up by the Romans on a hill called Golgotha, God punished Jesus with all the curses of the Torah. He became sin for us, like the scapegoat from the Day of Atonement ceremony in Leviticus 16. Since we violated all the Laws of the Torah, God placed all the curses of the Torah on Jesus.

In this way, Jesus freed us "from everything from which you could not be freed by the Law of Moses."[13] "There is therefore now no condemnation for those who are in Christ Jesus. For the Law of the Spirit of life has set you free in Christ Jesus from the Law of sin and death."[14]

Discussion Questions

• Where did Paul go first in Pisidian Antioch and why?

• Why might the synagogue leader have allowed Paul to speak?

• Who were the God-fearers?

• What did Paul say about the Sanhedrin and their role in Messiah's death?

• If Paul was anti-Torah and anti-Judaism how would his message in the synagogue have been different?

• What is wrong with urging Jewish believers in Jesus to give up their Jewish heritage?

• Why did Paul call it a tree instead of a cross?

Chapter 6
Beginning to Understand Galatians

I had just finished demonstrating the Passover and its connections to the Last Supper and the Lord's Supper when one of the deacons asked me, "Aren't you Judaizing? We're not under the Law."

From time to time people will assume that anyone who does anything Jewish is violating the teaching of Galatians. No book seems to challenge the Jewishness of Paul quite like Galatians.

According to popular interpretation, Paul had preached to the people of Galatia a Law-free gospel. Then some Messianic Jews had come along who had disturbed things, "Paul's teaching was good, but there is more if you want to go deeper. You need to start keeping the Law of Moses, beginning with circumcision."

Along this line, the church father Tertullian said, "They perverted the gospel in their teaching, not indeed by such a tampering with the Scripture as should enable them to expunge the Creator's Christ, but by so retaining the ancient régime as not to exclude the Creator's Law."[1] In other words, the Galatians did well to accept Christ, but they erred by failing to reject the Law.

Adam Clarke, a popular commentator referred to by many pastors in sermon preparation, says, "Christ … has taught us to renounce the Law, and expect justification through his death."[2] Clarke uses a strong word. Renounce is a word implying rejection. How can anyone say that Christ taught us to reject the Law when he clearly said, "I did not come to abolish the Law"?[3] He didn't come to abolish it but he wants us to reject it?

Jamieson, Fausset, and Brown, another popular commentary for pastors, paraphrases Galatians 2:18 as follows: "Since we have cast aside the

Law, thus having put ourselves in the same category as the Gentiles, who, being without the Law, are, in the Jewish view 'sinners,' is therefore Christ, the minister of sin?"[4] In other words, these scholars envision Paul saying to Peter, "You and I have cast aside the Law." When did Paul or Peter cast aside the Law in their own practice? The book of Acts does not in any way support this interpretation.

What would lead a church father and some very influential modern commentators to urge us: (1) to reject our Creator's Law, (2) to contradict Jesus by renouncing the Law, and (3) to contradict Acts by seeing Paul as a Law-breaker? Could it be that there is no problem with the Bible but only a problem with the Bible's interpreters?

Galatians 2:11-15: A Key to the Book

Suppose that in your church there were both Jews and Gentiles. Just imagine that we lived in a time where Jewish disciples roughly equaled the number of Gentile disciples. Further imagine that controversy broke out and the Jewish believers stopped eating with non-Jews.

Every time you had a church supper, you'd have to have two church suppers. If the pastor was Jewish, he wouldn't have lunch meetings with Gentiles or invite Gentiles to his home.

There is a story much like that in Galatians 2:11-21, a story about Peter, Barnabas, and the Jewish believers in Antioch. A kind of wrong-thinking existed about the place of Jews and Gentiles in the congregation. Paul used this story as an example of the same kind of error occurring among the Galatians.

Peter had become a hypocrite, at least in one way. Hypocrite is a term from Greek drama. The actors engaged in hypocrisy, pretending to be something they were not.

Peter's hypocrisy began when he started acting like a Jewish separatist, no longer eating with his Gentile friends. He was not really a separatist and had been eating with Gentiles for years. This might seem a strange issue to us, but in Peter's day it was a powder-keg.

God said in the Torah that contact with certain things made a person unclean until they were purified. Touching a corpse, an object with mildew, or unclean meat, for example, would make a person unclean.[5]

Many in Israel, such as the Pharisees, believed in what might be termed secondary separation. That is, not only were faithful Jews to avoid contamination by uncleanness, but they were also to avoid mingling with people who might be unclean.

It was not a sin to become unclean. It was a sin to fail to follow pre-scribed Laws to purify oneself from uncleanness. It was also a sin to bring uncleanness into sacred areas, such as the temple.

The Pharisees and other groups taught that Jews should not mix com-pany, especially in dining, with Gentiles. Gentiles did not avoid unclean meat. Gentiles did not purify themselves following menstruation, corpse contact, and other sources of uncleanness. A faithful Jew should avoid unclean people because their uncleanness could be caught.

Peter began dining with Gentiles following a vision in Acts 10. Using the imagery of unclean meat, God revealed to Peter that Gentiles are not unclean. Peter began dining with them, starting with Cornelius and his household. Later, this got Peter into trouble with some unidentified Jews referred to simply as "the circumcision."[6] They said to him, "You went to uncircumcised men and ate with them."[7]

Mixed dining with Gentiles became Peter's regular practice until an incident in Antioch, recorded in Galatians 2. There, some men came from James in Jerusalem. After their coming, Peter began to separate himself, eating only with Jews. Barnabas and the other Messianic Jews began to follow him in this hypocrisy. Paul opposed them all and called them to live the gospel.

What are we to make of this story? What could the men from James have told Peter that made him change his behavior? Peter's eating with Gentiles originated with a direct revelation from God. What could shake him from such a strong foundation?

According to popular interpretation, the men from James put pres-sure on Peter, feeling it unfit for a Jew to mix with Gentiles. The prob-lem in Antioch, this interpretation tells us, is that over-zealous Messianic Jews, led by James, wanted to separate the congregation. There are two major problems with this view.

First, James was sympathetic to Gentile inclusion in the congregations and would not send messengers to disrupt it. In the book of Acts James said, "Simeon has related how God first visited the Gentiles, to take from them a people for his name. And with this the words of the prophets agree."[8] Was James for or against Gentile inclusion? Obviously he was for it, so why would he have made a problem for Peter about it?

Second, Peter acted out of fear, not just peer pressure. Paul said that he feared the circumcision.[9] What was Peter afraid of? What made him act out of fear, not faith? What made him go against the revelation of God he received in Acts [10]?

No one can perfectly and with 100% confidence reconstruct the situation in Galatians 2. But we can make an educated guess that must be somewhat close to the truth.

The Reason for Peter's Fear

The fact is, Israel was headed toward rebellion against Rome. Things were heating up in Judea, Peter's home. Perhaps while Peter was up in Antioch in Syria, events had transpired back in Judea.

One of the growing movements of the time was the Zealots. One of Jesus' disciples, Simon the Zealot, came from this party.[10] The Zealots wanted to see a purified, Rome-free Israel. There is some evidence they might have persecuted and threatened Jews who mixed freely with Romans and Gentiles.[11]

Possibly what happened is that James sent messengers to let Peter know his life might be in danger when he returned to Judea. His mixing and mingling with Gentiles in Syrian Antioch, a major Jewish and Roman city, had been noticed. Peter, out of fear for his life, became something he was not: a Jewish separatist.

This interpretation better fits the facts. It explains why Peter was afraid. He wasn't afraid of James, his friend and fellow believer, but of Judean Zealots. It also explains why James sent him a message. James, brother of Jesus, was not a heretic, demanding that Gentiles be converted to Judaism in order to be saved. He simply wanted Peter to know of the danger.

Notice that the issue in Galatians 2 is not about keeping the Torah. The issue is Jewish separatism. Paul did not take a stand against the Torah, but against a man-made issue that would destroy the unity of the congregation of Jesus. Paul's example in Galatians 2 can prepare us to better understand the rest of Galatians.

Peter's Story and Ours

Admittedly, it is unlikely that your congregation will anytime soon experience a split between the Jews and Gentiles. Quite possibly there aren't even any Jewish people in your congregation.

Yet the principles Paul stood for against Peter in Antioch are very much relevant today. Paul was not in any way against Jewish practice or God's commandments. He was, however, against a false separation of people in the congregation.

If Jesus has made someone clean, do not regard them as unclean. Do not allow the opinions of others to keep you from unity with all other believers. People of different ethnic backgrounds, different levels of education, different levels of wealth, and different lifestyles are one in Jesus.

It would be wrong, however, to conclude from Galatians 2 that somehow Judaism or the commandments of Moses are a problem. Peter was not led astray by the Torah, which says nothing about avoiding interaction between Jews and Gentiles. He was led astray by the false, man-made separation imposed by hateful men.

Paul himself led a very Jewish life. He said to Peter, "If you, though a Jew, live like a Gentile and not like a Jew, how can you force the Gentiles to live like Jews?"[12]

What did Paul mean, that Peter no longer observed Jewish dietary Laws or saw himself as a Jew? Certainly not. Like Paul and James, Peter also remained a Jew his whole life. Paul meant that Peter did not act like a Jew in the sense of separating from Gentiles.

In teaching the Jewish background of our faith in numerous churches, I have had a few people ask me if I was Judaizing. Yet I have also experienced the opposite. One deacon in a Baptist church in Georgia said to me, "That makes sense. If Jesus was Jewish and a Jew believes in him, why should I or anyone else expect him to quit living a Jewish life?"

Absolutely, the enemy is not Leviticus. The enemy is not Jewish culture. The enemy is sin and man-made religion that contradicts God. This is the beginning of understanding Galatians. For just as the real issue in Antioch was not a problem with God's word to Moses, so the problem in Galatia was not either. The drama of Galatians is often misunderstood. Now we are prepared to unravel that drama and change the way we view Paul's letter to Galatia.

Discussion Questions

• What is the popular interpretation of Galatians?

• What did Tertullian say was the error of the Galatians?

• How had Peter been acting like a hypocrite in Antioch?

• Why didn't some religious Jews mix with Gentiles?

• Why did Peter fear the circumcision and separate from Gentiles?

• What two reasons argue against the idea that James and Messianic Jews put pressure on Peter to separate from Gentiles?

• How does the anti-Gentile prejudice of the first century relate to issues in the church today?

Chapter 7

Unraveling the Drama
of Galatians

Every good play has characters. Galatians could be looked at as a letter about a play we have not seen. We were not present in the first century to witness the players. We do not know what sort of people opposed Paul. We do not know the motives of these opponents of Paul. We have not heard their speeches or seen their acting. We can merely read Paul writing about their teachings to another set of players, the Galatian believers.

Who are the characters in the Galatians story? The common theory is that three groups are in view: (1) Paul, (2) the Galatians believers, and (3) some over-zealous Messianic Jews who want Gentiles to convert and be more Jewish. The basic conflict of the story is that group three wanted to make group one get circumcised and obey the Law of Moses. Many people have come up with a name for group three: the Judaizers.

Would it surprise you to know that the Bible never mentions Judaizers? The word is coined from Galatians 2:14 which speaks of Peter not Judaizing (in the Greek) or not living like a Jew. The word Judaize is a Greek way of saying live like a Jew. By that definition Paul, Peter, James, Jesus, and all the apostles were Judaizers. Already some problems can be seen in the common theory of the characters in the Galatians drama. Can we tell from Paul's letter who the characters really were?

To be sure the problem was a serious one: the unnamed opponents of Paul were causing Galatians believers to desert the God who had called them undeservedly to Messiah.[1] These false teachers were distorting the gospel, preaching a good news contrary to the one Paul had delivered.[2]

What was their perversion? Jamieson, Fausset, and Brown say,

"Though acknowledging Christ, they insisted on circumcision and Jewish ordinances and professed to rest on the authority of other apostles, namely, Peter and James."[3] Adam Clarke says, "It is not gospel, i.e. good tidings, for it loads you again with the burdens from which the genuine Gospel has disencumbered you."[4] Note that both commentators assume the common theory: Paul's opponents were Messianic Jews and the problem was obedience to the Law of Moses, which we are supposed to believe was abolished at the cross.

Facts About the Drama of Galatians

Does this fit the facts? Are the influencers of the Galatians really well-meaning Messianic Jews too confused to realize that the Law of Moses is obsolete in Messiah? Consider these facts about Paul's opponents:

The influencers want to dominate the Galatian believers (4:17).
The influencers are born according to the flesh, not the Spirit (4:29), in other words, they were not believers.
The influencers are troubling and unsettling the Galatians (5:10, 12).
The influencers want to make a good showing and boast (6:12, 13).
The influencers want to force circumcision (6:12).
The influencers want to avoid persecution for the cross (6:12).

Already a few of these facts don't fit the common theory of Galatians. Paul's opponents were born of the flesh and not the Spirit. They could not be Messianic Jews. Galatians 4:29 seems to be overlooked in the common theory or explained away. Most often it is assumed that 4:29 does not refer to the influencers themselves, but to Jews who are persecuting the influencers. This is convenient to maintain the theory that Messianic Jews are causing the problem, but the text suggests these people born of the flesh are persecuting the Galatians directly. This is a hint at a new theory of the players of this drama.

Another major hint is Galatians 6:12. According to the common theory, Messianic Jews pressured the Gentiles to convert to Judaism to avoid persecution for the sake of the cross. They feared Jewish Zealots who would oppose them mixing with Gentiles.

These Messianic Jews believe in the cross. This would mean they believe that the cross makes Gentiles clean, for the point of the cross is forgiveness. Yet while believing in the message of the cross, they don't want to suffer for what they believe. Thus, they are hypocrites, converting Gentiles even though they know better.

There could be a much better explanation of Galatians 6:12. Maybe the influencers opposing Paul do not believe the message of the cross. They do not want to be persecuted for the message of the cross because they do not believe it. Maybe Paul was speaking of the influencers in 4:29 when he says they were born according to the flesh. Maybe the problem is not Messianic Jews but local Jews who do not believe in Jesus.

Mark Nanos, in his excellent book *The Irony of Galatians*, suggests a much better cast for the drama of Galatians. Rather than a play involving Paul versus Torah-zealous Messianic Jews, Nanos suggest four important groups in this story: (1) Paul, (2) the Galatian believers (mostly Gentile), (3) Jewish proselytizers from the local synagogues, and (4) the Roman authorities who govern the region.

Nanos has added a whole new character to the play as well a modifying other characters. The Romans now figure into the story and the Jews are not Jesus-believers. How could this cast of characters explain the evidence of Paul's letter?

In Nanos' version of the play, there are three levels of social influence. The Galatian believers are the most marginal, at the bottom. Above them in social status are the Jewish leaders of the local synagogue, recognized by Rome as a permitted religion protected under Roman Law. And above the Jewish leaders are the Roman officials, who govern and allow Judaism by their whim and decree.

Knowing about the Roman imperial cult and its influence especially in Asia Minor adds a whole new dimension to understanding Galatians. All subjects of Galatia were required to demonstrate submission to the emperor. This submission was more than merely accepting governance, but also to publicly worship the civic gods of Rome.[5] Obviously, neither Jesus-followers nor Jews could in good conscience bow to Roman gods.

This was not an issue for Jews, who were exempt under a special status granted by Rome, *religio licita*.[6] Even Jewish believers in Jesus were exempt, since they were still Jews. The question was, what about these Gentiles who followed Jesus? Were they Jews? Were they exempt from imperial worship like Jews?

Now a convincing identity for the opponents of Paul becomes clear. The Jewish leaders sent representatives to the Galatian congregations with a message: convert or we'll not recognize you as Jewish and exempt from the imperial cult. These Jewish leaders were motivated by fear. If the Roman authorities found out that they were harboring a non-Jewish sect from the imperial cult Rome might persecute the synagogue or remove their exemption. These Jewish leaders might be asked to face persecution for the cross of Christ in which they did not even believe![7]

The Jewish leaders offered a simple solution: circumcise your Gentiles and we will consider them converts. Then we will look good to the Roman authorities as well as to other Jewish communities. Then you can keep following Paul and the good news of your Messiah and we will also be satisfied.

The only problem with this seeming win-win situation is that Paul recognizes it immediately as distorting the good news of the cross: Gentiles do not have to become Jews in order to be included in the commonwealth of Israel. Jesus has already provided for Gentiles by means of the cross. If Gentiles convert thinking that only conversion includes them in God's people, they are making an idol out of conversion. They are turning from Jesus to conversion as the answer to their need for salvation.

The Difference Between the Two Plays

In the common theory of Galatians, the play has a very different point than in the new theory. In the common theory we see:

1. A divided group of Jesus-followers, with James and the Messianic Jews divided against the Gentile disciples and Paul.
2. A hypocritical group of Messianic Jews, who believe in the cross but don't want to be persecuted for it.
3. A rejection of the validity of the commandments found in Genesis through Deuteronomy as being old and outdated.

To be sure, it is possible to believe in a version of the common theory without accepting number three. It is possible that the Messianic Jews were not wrong to believe in the importance of the Law, they were just wrong in making Gentiles get circumcised. That is, assuming that the opponents were Messianic Jews does not require us to believe that the Law is abolished.

In this modified common theory, the Messianic Jews were trying to make Gentiles follow Laws only applicable to Jews. They wanted to see Gentiles circumcised even though the Law only required Jews to be circumcised.

Yet even in this modified common theory, we are still left with a divided congregation of Jesus-followers and a hypocritical group of Messianic Jews.

In the new theory, however, the Jesus-believers, Jew and Gentile, are united but confused. They are persuaded by Jewish leaders that conversion is a good idea. They are beginning to think that Jesus plus Jewish conversion is the answer.

Will this theory fit the facts of the rest of Galatians? Does it explain the many things said about the influencers and their error?

The Message of Galatians: An Overview

I am proposing that Paul's opponents were Jewish proselytizers distorting the good news of Messiah. In particular, they were distorting one aspect of the good news that was central to Paul's mission to Gentiles: the sacrificial death of Jesus had opened the way for Gentiles to be included as full members of God's people.

How was this truth about Gentile inclusion evident from the good news of the cross? It may have been evident from many angles, but two in particular stand out: (1) Jesus' appointing Paul to the Gentiles and (2) the realization that with Jesus' death and resurrection the kingdom had begun.

First, Paul had been given a charge to go to the Gentiles to proclaim the kingdom of God.[8] Second, Paul had recognized on the road to Damascus that Jesus was the Messiah, and that the kingdom of God had already begun. Therefore, certain prophecies about the age of Messiah were already relevant. James, for example, saw the answer in Amos 9:12, "the nations [Gentiles] who are called by my name."[9] Gentiles in the Messianic Age would belong to God's people while still remaining Gentiles.

The message of Galatians, then, is not difficult to understand:

Galatians 1	I am surprised you are confused by these Jewish proselytizers and are deserting the gospel. My gospel came directly from Jesus.
Galatians 2	I did not get my gospel from the other apostles and in fact opposed Peter directly when he pretended to be a Jewish separatist out of fear. Separating Jews and Gentiles denies the power of

	the cross which made us dead to the condemnation of the Law.
Galatians 3	If you accept conversion, you are saying you can be saved by the Law, but all you will get is a curse. Jesus already took the curse of the Law on himself.
Galatians 4	Trying to be saved by the Law (i.e. conversion) is making yourself a slave. You used to be slave to pagan cult worship and now you are doing a similar thing making yourself a slave to a false view of the Law.
Galatians 5	Messiah set you free from the Law's penalty, so don't put yourself under it again by being converted. Continue in the Spirit, not in the flesh, that is, do not try to be saved by fleshly conversion, but keep letting God make you a Law-keeper by the Spirit.
Galatians 6	Do good, help one another, and don't trust in the flesh. Your so-called friends from the synagogue don't have your best interest in mind. God has already made you a new creation.

To see the truth of this brief outline of Galatians, it is important to understand some of Paul's specific phrases and teachings in Galatians:

- 1:6 "turning to a different gospel"—The different gospel was the idea that to be included in Israel the Gentiles needed conversion instead of just needing Messiah.
- 2:12 "the circumcision"—Often translated "the circumcision party," the word party is not in the Greek text. This is a broad term for the Jewish community, not for a conspiratorial group of Messianic Jews taking over the congregations with false teaching.
- 2:16 "justified by works of the Law"—This is a purpose the Law of Moses (Torah) never had. The Law of Moses expressed God's will for righteous living and for Israel's government. To be justi-

fied by the Torah would be to be saved by conversion and keeping the Laws rather than being saved by repentance and faith in God and his Messiah.

- 3:13 "curse of the Law"—This does not mean Torah is a curse or the Law is a burden. God specifically says the Law is not a burden in passages like Deuteronomy 30:11 and 1 John 5:3. The curse of the Torah is literally a curse for Israel as a nation if the Torah is not kept. The curses are found in Leviticus 26 and Deuteronomy 28.
- 3:13 "becoming a curse for us"—Messiah received the curses of the Torah on the cross. He suffered the penalty of sin (Torah-breaking) on Israel's behalf and thus started the kingdom and made redemption for Jew and Gentile.
- 3:19 "it [Torah] was added because of transgressions"—If God had only given the promise and not the commandments, we would not know how to live righteously. The Law was added to help us know how not to transgress.
- 3:25 "we are no longer under a guardian"—The guardian is used here as an image for the Law. The Greek word is *pedagogue*, a slave who taught manners and made sure boys attended school and did their work. Not being under the guardianship of the Law does not mean the teachings of the guardian are irrelevant, only that we are no longer under the guardian's discipline (penalty, curse).
- 3:28 "neither Jew nor Greek"—He does not mean it is unimportant to be Jewish or of any other heritage, just that it is not better to be one or the other. Just as male and female distinctions matter, so do Jewish/Gentile distinctions, but neither is superior or inferior.
- 4:3 "elementary principles"—Better translated elementary powers or spirits. Paul means that before redemption, we were enslaved by demonic powers in the sense of being led astray by them.
- 4:9 "weak and worthless elementary principles"—Paganism had them trapped before knowing Messiah in a system of fleshly worship. So too, trying to be saved by conversion in the flesh is another form of fleshly worship. Paul is not calling Torah weak and worthless, he is referring to all religious systems of fleshly worship, including conversion for salvation. Ironically, if these former pagans tried to be saved by Law-keeping, that would have more in common with their former paganism than with the Torah.
- 4:10 "days and months and seasons and years"—Apparently the Galatians had already begun capitulating to the Jewish prosely-

tizers by keeping Jewish days out of fear. Paul is not against Gentiles observing the Sabbath or holy days out of love for God, but they were doing it to escape the imperial cult. They were acting Jewish in order to be saved instead of knowing salvation is in Messiah. Paul mentions Jewish times, not because he is against the congregations keeping them, but because this was an example of how the Galatians were already caving in to the pressure.

- 4:21 "you who desire to be under the Law"—This does not mean it is bad to obey God's commandments from the Torah. They wanted to be under the Law as in becoming Jewish to be protected or saved under the Law. They wanted to be under the Law's umbrella and thus made part of God's people by works rather than faith.

- 4:29 "born according to the flesh"—Just as Ishmael was of the flesh (not of the promise), so the proselytizers were of the flesh and not the Spirit. They were trying to accomplish by the flesh what God had already done by the Spirit: make Gentiles part of God's people.

- 5:1 "do not submit again to a yoke of slavery"—The Torah is not slavery, but trying to be saved by Torah-keeping and conversion is slavery. Formerly they had been slaves to pagan worship. Now they were turning again to fleshly means to be saved.

- 5:3 "obligated to keep the whole Law"—They were fooling themselves, believing that by being circumcised and doing their best to obey God's commandments they could be accepted. If they wanted an alternative way to be saved, conversion instead of faith in Messiah, they would have to perfectly keep Torah or face the curse of Torah. The only way out of Torah's curse is through the one who already took it upon himself.

Galatians is no anti-Judaism book, but an argument for one people of God, Jew and Gentile, accepted into God's people by faith. There are no second-class believers or twice-blessed believers. There are only people set free from the penalty of sin and joined together in one united community.

The Holy Spirit and Torah

There is something very liberating about Galatians if we will read it correctly. I've heard some good sermons that got that point. I remember hearing a pastor say something to this effect, "When you understand that you are not under condemnation, when you grasp that God accepts you as you are and is working to make you better, then you will know freedom." If anything, this is the point we should get from Galatians. It is not that God is against commandments and holiness, but that he accepts us and makes us holy by his power.

In Galatians 5:18 Paul says, "If you are led by the Spirit, you are not under the Law." By now it should be clear that being under the Law is not a reference to God's commandments as holy and good but to being under the condemnation of the Law.

This is borne out by the verses that follow. For Paul says, "walk by the Spirit and you will not gratify the desires of the flesh."[10] The works of the flesh are transgressions against God's Law. Paul is essentially saying, "Walk in the empowerment of the Spirit and you will not go around breaking the Law."

In case anyone doubts this connection, Paul describes the desires of the flesh: "sexual immorality, impurity, sensuality, idolatry, sorcery, enmity, strife, jealousy, fits of anger, rivalries, dissensions, divisions, envy, drunkenness, orgies, and things like these."[11]

What is the source of Paul's list? Why did he choose these particular sins to mention? It would seem they are a combination of two things: commandments from the Torah and particular sins to which pagans were prone.

The Torah has much to say about sexual immorality, impurity, and the kind of sins involved in orgies. Also, the Torah forbids many times idolatry and related practices such as sorcery. The list from enmity to divisions is forbidden by Torah Laws regarding love of neighbor and even love for enemies. Envy is the subject of the tenth commandment. The only vice on the list not easily tied to the Torah is drunkenness.

What Paul is saying is not that the Law should be rejected now that we have the Spirit. Some people get the idea that with the Spirit we no longer need commandments or written revelation. After all, some would say, the Spirit will reveal truth and will convict you of sin. This is not a minor point, but a major one.

What happens to our motivation to read, study, and memorize scripture if we believe that commandments are not helpful to holiness? Can we really get help in living right by reading commandments? Some would say, now that we have the Spirit, the commandments (from anywhere in the Bible) are weak and useless. The Spirit's guidance will help us without needing to study and memorize rules.

The simple refutation to this is that Paul and other New Testament writers obviously didn't agree, since they wrote numerous commandments for us to follow. If commandments are unhelpful then why did Paul spend so much time writing commandments?

And the Spirit is the one behind the scriptures. The Holy Spirit is not opposed to Torah, scripture, and commandments. He wrote them. They are his work and part of his empowerment to lead us to righteousness.

What Paul is saying is that the Spirit will empower us to follow commandments, including those in the Torah. By becoming sensitive to the Spirit's work inside us we will be better commandment-keepers, rather than commandment-rejecters.

It was vital for Paul to clear up this point for his Galatian audience. In urging them to reject the forced conversion of the synagogue prose-lytizers, Paul never wanted them to get the idea that Torah was not for them.

Ironically, this is the very message churches have too often derived from the book of Galatians. Forget about commandments and Laws and just be spiritual. Paul commands, however, walk "by the Spirit and you will not gratify the desires of the flesh." In other words, living in the power of the Holy Spirit will keep us from breaking God's commandments. And where are God's commandments to be found? They are all through the Bible, from Genesis to Revelation.

Discussion Questions

- Who were the influencers trying to force circumcision on Galatian Gentiles?
- What was the motivation of these influencers? Who were they afraid of and why?
- What hints are there that the influencers were not believers?
- How did Paul know that the good news of Messiah means full inclusion of Gentiles?
- Who was "the circumcision"?
- What is the curse of the Law and what does it have to do with Jesus?
- Does no longer being under the guardianship of the Law mean not needing to obey it? Why or why not?
- What does Paul call weak and worthless in 4:9?
- How would Galatians converting to Judaism be obligated to keep the whole Torah?
- What role do the Spirit and the commandments play in our holiness?

Chapter 8
Romans–Israel and the Gentiles

I sat in the back seat of a friend's station wagon, a friend who was also a mentor. Paul Diamond and I had been visiting homes and sharing with people about the way of Jesus.

If I had been confused before, I was even more confused now. Having been following Jesus for only a few months, I was already noticing the Jewishness of the New Testament and the lack of Jewishness in church services. I was also thinking that few if any Jewish people believed in this Jewish Messiah. The result for me was confusion about the validity of my newfound faith.

My newfound mentor had just thrown me another curve, a new one. When I shared my concerns with him, he laughed and said, "Derek, didn't you know? I'm Jewish."

A thousand thoughts struggled in my mind to get out. Paul Diamond? Jewish? But he believed in Jesus. I'd heard him many times tell people about Jesus. He couldn't be Jewish, could he?

Paul related to me how natural it was for a Jewish person to believe in a Jewish Messiah, a new thought for me. It fit with what I was already thinking about the Jewishness of the New Testament.

I'll never forget what happened next. Paul opened the Bible and took me to a chapter I'd never read before: Romans 11.

In Romans 11, the Apostle Paul painted a picture of an olive tree. This olive tree was a cultivated tree, producing crops year after year. The gardener in the picture Paul painted was busy doing something. He was grafting onto this olive tree branches from another variety, a wild olive tree.

Paul Diamond helped me see: this was a picture of the congregation of Messiah: the natural branches are Israel, physical Israel. The wild branches are Gentiles. The wild branches do not become natural branches, but they do join into the life of the tree. The roots are Jewish roots,[1] even if the wild branches should ever come to outnumber the natural ones.

I cannot begin to describe the lofty thoughts this image brought to my mind. I saw that something very ancient was behind the modern veneer of the faith. The world of church seemed very modern and unmystical. People a lot like me came to a place that was, honestly, mundane. Yet behind it all, there really was something ancient, a whole history of God's dealings with Israel.

A mystery was being revealed to me and my life has never been the same. I count that night as a turning point for me. There would be no turning away from my passion to learn about Judaism and Jesus. And the book that inspired it all was Romans.

The Jewishness of Romans

Imagine my surprise when I took a class on Romans in Bible College. What had at first seemed to me a book about Jews and Gentiles seemed anything but in the class. We talked class period after class period about justification, sanctification, and salvation by grace. I heard or read someone during that course of time saying that Romans differed from all of Paul's other writings in being more like pure theology without some problem or issue being addressed. Being the longest of Paul's letters and having many theological sections, I'm not surprised that people might feel that way about Romans. Yet even on a simple reading, it is obvious that there is some issue about Jews and Gentiles behind the book.

The thesis of the book already hints at some underlying issue, saying that the message of the good news is "to the Jew first and also to the Greek."[2] Then, as Paul sets out to demonstrate the sinful condition of all humankind, he argues separate cases for Gentile idolatry[3] and Jewish nomism.[4] If we haven't already gotten a clue to the agenda of Romans, Paul digresses at the beginning of chapter 3 to explain the advantages of being Jewish. The issue of Jews and the Law keeps coming up throughout the book, coming to a climax in chapters 9-11.

Something had happened in Rome. The Jesus-followers there clearly needed some instruction about Jews, Gentiles, and the true message of Jesus. Romans is far from pure theology. Paul, inspired by the unseen

Spirit, shapes this book to address issues vital to the congregations in Rome, Jewish-Gentile issues to be sure.

The Weak and the Strong: A Major Clue

Believe it or not, one of the strongest clues that will lead us to the real issue behind Romans comes from a passage thought difficult to understand: Romans 14:1—15:13.

Paul speaks here of the weak and the strong. Many commentators are quick to decide what the issue is here: the strong are Gentile disciples who believe in freedom from the Law. The weak are Jewish disciples who erroneously continue to practice Jewish distinctives from the Law, such as avoiding unclean meat. What Paul is trying to do is get the strong to go easy on the weak even though they supposedly are closer to the truth.

Mark Nanos, a Jewish scholar whose theory on Galatians thoroughly persuaded me,[5] tackles conventional readings of Romans and proposes a new theory.[6]

There are a few problems with the conventional theory that the weak are Jewish disciples and the strong are Gentile disciples. First, if the weak are simply wrong, thinking they should still have a Jewish relationship to the Law, keeping the practices given exclusively for Israel, then why doesn't Paul teach them the error of their ways?[7] Further, Romans 1-11 does not reflect a dispute between Jewish and Gentile colleagues in the congregation so much as misinformation about the place of non-believing Jews in God's plan.[8] Also, we have seen from Paul's own life and practice that he was a Jew who continued practicing Jewish distinctives. Yet Paul did not consider himself weak.

Nanos's theory, which better suits the facts, is that the weak were non-believing Jews. They were weak because they didn't believe in the cross. They could not be persuaded that Gentiles do not have to live as Jews because they had no belief in a savior for Jew and Gentile. The idea that God would accept Gentiles without requiring them to keep Jewish distinctives (dietary Laws, holy days, circumcision, etc.) was foreign to them.

The strong were both Gentile and Jewish disciples, who knew that Gentiles are accepted into God's people without becoming Jews. Paul, a Jew who kept dietary Laws and calendar observances, was strong because he knew it was acceptable for Gentiles not to follow suit.

In fact, Paul is not commending the strong for their behavior and attitudes.[9] He is challenging them. If they want to see Jewish people in Rome come to faith in Jesus, they should not offend by ridiculing Jewish obser-vances or flaunting their practice of eating differently and keeping their calendar differently. They should not "destroy the one for whom Christ died."[10]

The situation at Rome must have involved some level of interaction between the disciples and the Jewish community. This interaction may have involved disparaging words toward Jews. Romans were in the habit of ridiculing Jewish practices, especially dietary Laws and Sabbath observance.[11]

What can be learned from this, as well as other evidence, is that Romans was written to explain the place of Jews and Gentiles in God's plan. Romans was written to a community with tensions between the disciples and the Jewish community. Romans was written to increase the appreciation of the disciples for God's plan and purpose for Israel.

Tensions Between Disciples and Jews in Rome

Suetonius (c. 75—160) was a secretary to the emperor Hadrian and is known for his writings about the lives of the Caesars. In his *Life of Claudius*, the Roman historian records that the emperor "expelled the Jews from Rome because they were constantly arguing at the instigation of Chrestus."[12]

We cannot be sure, but Chrestus may well be a misspelling of Christ. It is likely, for reasons that will become clear, that this incident recorded by the Roman writer has bearing on the book of Romans.

In Acts 18:2, Luke tells the story of Paul meeting Priscilla and Aquila, two Jewish disciples[13] who had just come from Rome "because Claudius had commanded all the Jews to leave Rome." The story of Acts 18 and the incident recorded in Suetonius are likely to refer to the same inci-dent. This expulsion of Jews from Rome during Claudius' time is further confirmed in a fifth-century historian, Orosius, and to some degree by a second-century historian, Dio Cassius.[14]

Later, probably after the death of Claudius in 54 C.E., the Jews came back. For example, in Romans 16:3-4, Paul refers to Priscilla and Aquila being back in Rome with a congregation meeting in their house.

Understanding the timing is crucial to seeing the picture behind the book of Romans. The Jews were expelled around 49 C.E. Romans was written around 57 C.E. The Jewish disciples had been back at the most three years, having been gone for five.

Consider the effects an expulsion of many or all of the Jews from

Rome would have had on the congregations. Almost certainly the congregations at Rome, as elsewhere, began with Jewish disciples and Gentile God-fearers. Then, from around 49 until 54 C.E., they all had to leave. What started as a Jewish institution became a Jewish vacuum.

Consider further the fact that the Jewish disciples had to leave Rome because of arguments that must have become riots if the emperor took notice. This means that the Jewish leaders in Rome had caused pain to the congregations.[15] There were sources of tension between these two communities, the Jesus-followers and the Jewish residents of Rome.

This tension is the reason Paul wrote the book of Romans. Paul wrote to explain the relationship of Israel and the followers of Jesus, to be an ambassador for the Jewish people to the congregations, and to commend the recently returned Jewish disciples in Rome.

Why would Paul need to be an ambassador for the Jews? Not only were there tensions evident from the expulsion during the time of Claudius. There were also tensions in general between Romans and Jews. Certainly the Jews had rights and privileges that were unique and which were upheld throughout the empire by the emperors. Yet the Jews were regarded by many Romans as backwards.

Idolatry was central to all elements of Roman society. In all the customs of the people, elements of idol worship were mixed in to such a degree that Jews could not participate in Roman society. In his book Paganism and the Roman Empire, R. MacMullen observes:

> For most people, to have a good time with their friends involved
> some contact with a god who served as the guest of honor, as
> master of ceremonies, or as host in the porticoes or flowering,
> shaded grounds of his own dwelling. For most people, meat was
> a thing never eaten and wine to surfeit never drunk save as
> some religious setting permitted.[16]

Not only could Jewish people not eat in a setting involving honoring household and civic gods, but wine and meat were very much a part of Jewish life. The Jewish community was socially isolated from Roman society.

On top of this, Romans thought of Jews as superstitious because their religious practices were so different. In particular, dietary Laws and Sabbath observances were ridiculed. Juvenal, a second-century writer, said that Sabbath observance proved the Jews to be lazy in his *Satire*

14:96-106. A rumor also started that the Jews never showed their God because they were embarrassed. Supposedly he had the head of a donkey.[17]

In an atmosphere where there had been tensions between Jews and Romans, Paul tells the Roman disciples:

> Then what advantage has the Jew? Or what is the value of circumcision? Much in every way. To begin with, the Jews were entrusted with the oracles of God.[18]

Paul says, "So the Law is holy, and the commandment is holy and righteous and good."[19] Of Israel he says:

> They are Israelites, and to them belong the adoption, the glory, the covenants, the giving of the Law, the worship, and the promises. To them belong the patriarchs, and from their race, according to the flesh, is the Christ who is God over all, blessed forever. Amen. . . . Brothers, my heart's desire and prayer to God for them is that they may be saved. . . . all Israel will be saved.[20]

Paul is an ambassador, representing Israel to the Romans and promoting the true gospel: Jew and Gentile together in unity in Messiah.[21]

Paul's Program to Explain and Promote Israel

Virtually every part of Romans can be understood in light of this purpose: to explain the place of Jews and Gentiles in God's plan and to promote Israel in the eyes of the Roman disciples:

Romans 1	Gospel to Jew first and to Greek. The guilt of Gentile pagans before God proven.
Romans 2	A self-righteous Gentile shown guilty and a self-righteous Jewish teacher set straight.
Romans 3	Advantage of the Jew, guilt of Jew and Gentile, God's free gift to Jew and Gentile.
Romans 4	A Jewish case, from Torah, for Jew and Gentile united under Abrahamic promise.

Romans 5	All humankind (Jew and Gentile) can be reconciled through second Adam, for Adam is father of all humankind.
Romans 6	Does our forgiveness mean irrelevance of Law? By no means.
Romans 7	Law's condemnation cannot effect us, and Law cannot make us do right.
Romans 8	New promise is more than the Law, Spirit power to fulfill the Law. This begins now and will continue into the life to come where we'll be made perfect.
Romans 9	Gentiles' non-election as Chosen People explained and Israel's current unbelief explained.
Romans 10	God is not through with Israel, and the task of all disciples is to see God's plan for Israel through, teaching the good news to all.
Romans 11	God has not rejected Israel. Israel's unbelief part of God's plan. Gentiles brought into God's blessings on Israel should respect the root of the Olive Tree into which they are grafted.
Romans 12	Even for Gentiles there is a sacrifice. Let no one be arrogant. Love and bless so the congregation will be united.
Romans 13	Be good citizens and walk godly before the Roman world.
Romans 14	The strong (disciples) know that Gentiles do not have to live as Jews, but do not flaunt this and keep weak (non-believing Jews) from faith by your arrogance.
Romans 15	Live for your neighbor, including the non-believing Jew, for Messiah served both Jew and Gentile.
Romans 16	Personal greetings including commending Jewish disciples (Prisca and Aquila, Andronicus and Junia, Aristobulus, Herodion).

Paul's greatest defense of the Jewish people comes in chapters 9-11. Paul's passion for Israel and his incredible grasp of the marvels of God's plan are beautifully displayed. Yet even here, few grasp the full import of Paul's words. God's plan for the world is Israel-centered. This is a truth Christianity must learn and embrace.

Romans on Israel

Reading Romans 9-11 is much easier when you understand the issues behind the text.

Paul begins with an incredible statement in 9:1-3: he would be willing to be cursed by God and put out of the congregation of Messiah if that sacrifice would save his fellow Israelites. Imagine if Christian churches began to long for Israel's fulfillment as Paul did. Paul's argument continues:

9:4-5	Israel is glorious and beloved by God.
9:6-13	God did not choose Israel for nothing and his plan did not fail. Always in God's plan only part of the line received the blessing. We should not be surprised now that only some in Israel believe.
9:14-18	Does this mean God is unjust? He has his own reasons, beyond our knowledge, for his choosing and his rejection. He chose Israel and not other nations.
9:19-24	If God is just going to choose whoever he wants, why should we try? You cannot blame God. He has been patient with unrighteous Israel and Gentiles, destined for destruction, in order to show mercy to his full people, both Jews and Gentiles, who believe.
9:25-29	The prophets foretold both that Gentiles would be included and many in Israel would be lost.
9:30-33	Is it the Law that kept many in Israel out? Did lack of Law save Gentiles? No, it is that Israel did not perceive the purpose of the Law, but made it an end in itself.

10:1-4	I yearn for Israel to be saved, but they sought God through their own righteousness. They did not see that the goal (telos, end) of the Law was Messiah. He is what it always pointed to.
10:5-13	For Moses and the prophets explained the true way. Moses should be understood as saying that salvation comes from God, not from achievement. Joel shows that asking for God's aid is the basis for salvation.
10:14-17	But your attitude to the Jews will not do, for they cannot be saved unless you reach out to them.
10:18-21	God's ways often confound us, for he saves the unworthy that the arrogant may see and be humbled.
11:1-6	Israel is still God's Chosen People, and even at the present we see a remnant of Jewish disciples as in Elijah's day.
11:7-10	God is not defeated by unbelieving Israel. Those foreordained obtained it and the rest didn't. There has always been a chosen remnant.
11:11-16	Most of Israel missed it and God poured his blessing out on new people, who will in turn make them jealous. When Israel comes back, the miracle will be even greater: life from the dead (resurrection).
11:17-24	You have been included in Israel's blessings, so don't be arrogant. The Jewish root supports you.
11:25-27	Don't be arrogant regarding the Jews, for a time will come when all Israel living at that time will be saved, just as God said in the prophets.
11:28-32	Right now the Jews may oppose you, but remember you were once God's enemies also. Yet God allows all disobedience to continue, just as he allowed yours in the past and theirs now, because he gives all the opportunity to receive mercy.

Probably the strongest and clearest message comes in verses 28 and 29. Some commentators persist in trying not to get the message of Romans 11. Israel, some say, refers not to Jews by physical descent, but all followers of Jesus. John Calvin, for example, said about Israel in verse 26, "Many understand this of the Jewish people, as though Paul had said, that religion would again be restored among them as before: but I extend the word Israel to all the people of God."[22]

That Paul is addressing physical Israel is clear from verses 28 and 29. He uses the pronoun they, referring back to verses 26 and 27. The people of whom he speaks are the same as in verse 26. Yet he says of them "as regards the gospel, they are enemies." This is physical Israel, non-believing Israel. And yet what does Paul say of them? He says, "they are beloved for the sake of their forefathers." His promise from verse 26 stands out even more when it is clear that physical Israel is meant — "all Israel will be saved."

Paul's love for Israel and his sense of Israel in God's plan is deep. He points the Gentile disciples to a realization of Israel's place: beloved though not-yet believing, children of promise though at present rejecting Messiah. Paul is saying to the congregation (and to the modern church): know and respect Israel, for they are God's people and will never be rejected!

Romans on the Torah

It is in light of Paul's purpose in Romans that we can best understand his many statements about the Law, meaning the Law of Moses or the Torah:

- Romans 2:12—Both Jews and Gentiles are guilty, for those without the Law (Gentiles) will be judged by God's righteousness (which is behind the Law) and those under the Law (Jews) will be judged by the Law itself.
- Romans 2:13—Hearing a commandment doesn't make you righteous. Doing a commandment is righteousness.
- Romans 2:15—You can see behind the Law the wisdom of God which all humankind carries in the conscience.
- Romans 2:17—You, hypothetical Jewish teacher, think that just by being of the people to whom the Law was given have a right standing with God, but you are deceived.
- Romans 2:23—You are not saved by belonging to the people who

received the Law. When you break that Law, you prove your guilt.

- Romans 2:25—Your status as a Jew (circumcision) is not enough by itself.
- Romans 3:19—The purpose of the Law is to show the guilt of humankind.
- Romans 3:20—The Law was never meant to save.
- Romans 3:21—The Law and prophets pointed to Messiah and are consistent with Messiah.
- Romans 3:31—Don't think this means the Law is irrelevant. We uphold the Law as God's standard. His commandments are relevant.
- Romans 4:13—God's promise to Jew and Gentile came before the Law and transcends it.
- Romans 5:20—Knowing the Law increases guilt, since the Law more perfectly shows God's will than mere conscience.
- Romans 6:14—You are not under Law, i.e. not judged by it, therefore you have a new power to be free from sin.
- Romans 6:15—Not being judged by the Law is no excuse to break it. Freedom from condemnation is not license to sin.
- Romans 7:2—In order to be set free from the Law's condemnation, you had to die mystically through Messiah's death.
- Romans 7:6—When the Law was merely a written code it had no power to help you keep it. But you live in the Spirit, who helps you keep God's commandments.
- Romans 7:14—The problem was never the Law, which is spiritual. The problem was always our flesh which rebels against God.
- Romans 7:22—The Law excites my spirit, for I know it to be the truth and the way of God.
- Romans 8:2—In Messiah you are set free from the Law's death ministry.
- Romans 8:4—Now life in the Spirit does not look like Lawlessness, but like empowered Law-keeping.
- Romans 8:7—Opposition to the Law of Moses is fleshly, not spiritual.

In spite of clear statements like, "the Law is spiritual," in Romans 7:14, Christian interpreters continue to interpret Paul as being against the Torah. Douglas Moo says the weak in Romans 14 were "Jewish Christians . . . who believed that they were still bound by certain 'ritual' requirements of the Mosaic Law."[23] Witherington agrees that "Judaism is an extant form of religion that Paul left behind when he had his

...nascus Road experience. Christ came to redeem those under the Law, ...ut from under that Law."[24]

Would that Christianity would hear Paul's true message! Paul the Pharisee and Torah-observant Jew did not oppose the Torah's validity for Jesus-followers. Paul simply taught that Gentiles did not need to become Jews in order to be right with God. Also, Jews are not saved because they belong to the people who received the Law. The Law is a revelation of God's righteousness, but in itself has no power to save. Therefore, let all who love the Lord obey his Law, Jews as Jews (including commandments exclusive to Israel) and Gentiles as Gentiles. After all, we uphold the Law of Moses and fulfill it by the Spirit.

Discussion Questions

• What does Paul's picture of the Olive Tree in Romans 11 say about Jews and Gentiles in the congregation?

• What is the conventional theory about the weak and the strong in Romans 14?

• What are some problems with the conventional theory?

• What theory does Mark Nanos propose about the weak and the strong?

• What did the Emperor Claudius do that affected Jewish-Gentile relationships in Rome?

• What is Paul's basic purpose in Romans?

• Why are Messianic Jews singled out in Romans 16 in the greetings?

• How do Romans 11:28-29 prove that Romans 11:26 refers to Jews by physical descent?

• How does Romans 6:14-15 inform your view of a believer's relationship to the Law?

Chapter 9
Ephesians 2–One New Man

Sometimes, verses that we think mean one thing end up leading us in a completely different direction. This happens quite often with Paul and the Law, because Paul's issues with the Law were very different from ours.

In Paul's day, the Law was used by certain Jewish groups in wrong ways. Many in Israel believed that the whole nation was saved through the giving of the Law. Individual Jews simply needed to basically adhere to the Law in order to be included. This was a very different issue from the later problem of people believing God saves those who become perfect in obedience (Pelagianism as the theologians call it).

Also, in Paul's day, the Law was misused to attempt to force Gentiles to convert, saying that conversion plus Jesus is necessary for a Gentile to be saved. By the same terms, some dominant Jewish groups held that Jews and Gentiles should not mix socially. Herod and the Sadducees put up a barrier to keep Gentiles out of the temple's inner court, for example.

Perhaps it is because of the different set of issues confronting Paul in his time versus the issues of our time that so many of his statements on the Law are misread. A case in point is Ephesians 2:15.

In Ephesians 2:15, Paul speaks of Messiah "abolishing the Law of commandments and ordinances." This verse is taken by most commentators as the exact opposite of Matthew 5:17.

Jesus said, "Do not think that I have come to abolish [*kataluo*] the Law," yet Paul says that in his death Jesus was "abolishing [*katargaysas*] the Law of commandments and ordinances." Although the two Greek words are not exactly the same, their meaning is very similar. This is as close to a contradiction as you can get.

In fact, if Ephesians 2:15 is interpreted in this way, with Messiah abolishing the Torah, then Paul also contradicts himself. In Romans 3:31

asks, "Do we then overthrow [katargoumen] the Law by this faith?" His answer is, "By no means!" Here the word overthrow is the exact same Greek verb as Ephesians 2:15. Thus, in one text Paul says our faith does not abolish the Torah and in the other he says it does.

What is Paul saying? Is he against the Torah as a relevant book for disciples of Jesus?

As a further clue to this mystery, consider the way Paul uses the Torah in Ephesians. In a passage admonishing children to obey their parents, Paul refers to the Torah itself, noting that this is a commandment with a promise.[1] How can Paul say the Torah is abolished and then quote it with authority? In fact, he takes literally the promise of Exodus 20:12 about obeying parents "that your days may be long in the land that the Lord your God is giving you."

If Paul is to mean in Ephesians 2:15 that the Torah is abolished in the death of Messiah then he must:

1. Contradict Jesus in Matthew 5:17.
2. Contradict himself in Romans 3:31.
3. Contradict his own use of Torah in Ephesians 6:2.

Perhaps Paul's meaning is actually something different. Perhaps his meaning will be clarified by the context of the letter of Ephesians itself.

Jew and Gentile Together in Messiah

Paul's concern in Ephesians is to develop the implications of the unity of all believers in Messiah. He refers numerous times to issues of unity:

1:13	In him you also . . . were sealed with the promised Holy Spirit,
1:22-23	the church [*ekklesia*, gathering], which is his body
2:4-5	But God . . . made us alive together with Christ
2:11-12	at one time you Gentiles in the flesh . . . were at that time separated from Christ
2:13	once were far off have been brought near
2:14	has made us both one
2:15	create in himself one new man in place of the two

Specifically the unity Paul is at pains to demonstrate is between Jew and Gentile. Paul wants the believers in Ephesus to know that they share in the same blessings as the original Jewish disciples and even the apostles themselves.

We may never know Paul's exact reason for emphasizing the unity of Jew and Gentile in the congregation of Messiah. Was he merely expressing the beauty of God's plan of reconciliation as an exercise in praise? Had there been some disunity which Paul was addressing? Had the Ephesian believers, like the Galatians, become concerned that being Gentile was not good enough? If there was a controversy, Ephesians is remarkably calm compared to Galatians.

Yet, whatever his exact reason, Paul is addressing the unity of Jew and Gentile in the body of Messiah in Ephesians 2. It is in this context that Ephesians 2:15 must be read. To understand the meaning of this significant verse, it is import to follow Paul's chain of thought throughout the chapter:

2:1	You used to be dead to God through your sins, but have been made alive.
2:2	You used to be under the influence of Satan.
2:3	We all, even us Jews, used to be under the same influence and destined for wrath.
2:4-7	Yet it was God's mercy to make us alive, guarantee our resurrection, and give us a heavenly identity awaiting the Messianic Age when we will be fully revealed.
2:8-9	Don't think that any of us earned it, it was by undeserved favor from God.
2:10	Your good works have another purpose, not to save you but to please him.
2:11	Remember that you were once outsiders.
2:12	Remember that you were once not of God's people.
2:13	Now by Messiah's death you have been included.
2:14	For he has included Gentiles along with Jews.
2:15	To bring us together he had to abolish "the Law of commandments in statutes" in order to make one new man.

What could Paul's point be, that Jesus had to abolish to Torah so Jews and Gentiles could be together? If so, what about the Torah kept Jews and Gentiles apart?

Many commentators quote a second century B.C.E. letter by Aristeas to make this exact point. Andrew Lincoln, for example, says:

> Torah itself could be seen as providing a fence around Israel. In the second century B.C.E. the *Epistle of Aristeas* declared: "our Lawgiver ... fenced us about with impenetrable palisades of iron to the end that we should mingle in no way with any of the other nations, remaining pure in body and spirit" (139).[2]

Certainly there did exist a common Jewish interpretation of the Torah that forbade social contact between Jews and Gentiles. However, would Jesus abolish the God-given Torah because of a prevalent false interpretation?

Though Aristeas and many other Jews may have seen avoidance of Gentiles as legislated by Torah, the Torah itself does not share this value. Numerous verses like Exodus 12:49 envision foreigners living in the land sharing the same justice as native-born. A careful study of the tabernacle regulations will reveal that foreigners were allowed in Torah to come to the altar and offer sacrifices.[3] There is a widespread misconception that Jews were forbidden to marry Gentiles in the Torah. The truth is they were forbidden to marry Canaanites[4] and idolaters.[5]

Interaction between Jews and Gentiles occurs at many levels in the Hebrew Bible. Elijah and Elishah lived in the home of a widow in Zarephath, a Phoenician town. Naaman the Syrian came to Elisha and found favor with him. Moses' two wives were a Midianite and a Cushite.

If the Torah does not forbid or diminish social interaction between Jews and Gentiles, where is the problem that Messiah had to address? Many are led astray by considering Jewish interpretations of Torah rather than the Torah itself.

In the interpretation of many Jewish sects, the Sadducees,[6] Pharisees,[7] and Essenes[8] fraternizing with Gentiles spread impurity and could lead to defilement. The temple itself, rebuilt and enlarged by Herod, had a fence keeping Gentiles out from the inner courts. An unwary interpreter might assume that this second-temple practice had the sanction of the Torah. Actually, it was a violation, one of many, of Torah.

Numbers 15:14 says, "And if a stranger is sojourning with you, or anyone is living permanently among you, and he wishes to offer a food offering, with a pleasing aroma to the Lord, he shall do as you do." In other words, just like you, Israelite, the foreigner shall come to the altar in the inner court and present his animal for the offering.

It was not the Torah that kept Jews and Gentiles apart. It was something else, something for which Messiah died.

What Did Jesus Abolish?

Markus Barth notes the problem of assuming that Ephesians 2:15 means the abolishment of the Torah:

> Paul's polemics against justification by Law. . . all such elements appear to suggest that the Law which is "abolished" according to Ephesians 2:15 is the holy Law of God. But in Romans 3:31; 7:22; 13:8-10 Paul flatly contradicts this opinion. "Do we thus abrogate the Law by faith? Far be it! On the contrary, we uphold the Law" . . . Either Paul is inconsistent and his teaching paradoxical, or Ephesians 2:15 must be understood as referring to something different from an invalidation of the revelation given to Moses on Mount Sinai.[10]

Barth goes on to give four alternative ways of understanding Ephesians 2:15:

1. The emphasis on commandments and statutes means that only some of the Laws of Torah are abolished (i.e. the ceremonial and civil).
2. The emphasis may be on statutes [*dogmata*], which could be a word for extra-biblical Laws ordained by rabbinic teachers and not the Torah itself.
3. The emphasis on commandments and statutes may have in view the Torah as a death sentence.
4. One of the Law's effects may be in view here: the Law, allegedly, promoted separation between Jews and Gentiles by making Israel separate from the nations. Only this Torah-sanctioned separation of Israel is in view.[11]

Regarding the first alternative, that Paul means the ceremonial Law has been abolished, Barth observes "the distinction between moral and ceremonial Laws cannot be upheld. Neither the Bible, nor the history of ḡions, nor sound theological reasons support it."[12]

Regarding the second option, that the rabbinic Laws and traditions were abolished in Messiah's death, this view could not possibly be what Paul had in mind. It is true that traditions rather than Torah commandments were causing the problem of Jew-Gentile separation. Concerns about contagious impurity and keeping Gentiles out of the inner courts of the temple all came from tradition, not Torah. Yet this cannot be what Paul has in mind, as elegant a solution as it would be, for there is no logic in saying Messiah had to die to abolish commandments which never had divine authority!

The fourth option, that Paul meant only the doctrine of the Torah that Israel is separate from the nations, has possibilities, but also fails the test. Deuteronomy 33:4 calls the Torah a "possession for the assembly of Jacob." Israel is called a holy nation, a separated nation, in Exodus 19:6. If Messiah removed this distinction in his death and caused Gentiles to fully share in Israel's election, that would logically fit Paul's argument. Furthermore, this interpretation is buttressed by New Testament teachings such as 1 Peter 2:9 which call Gentiles also a priesthood like Israel.

However, the problem with this view is two-fold: (1) Paul specifically says the abolishment has something to do with commandments and statutes, not a doctrine, and (2) God has not eliminated Israel's status as a holy nation. As Paul says in Romans 11:29, "The gifts and the calling of God are irrevocable."

It is the third option that ends up having the least problems. Messiah died to cancel the death sentence against us recorded in the Torah's commandments and statutes. The advantage of this view is multiple: (1) it fits with Paul's death imagery earlier in the chapter, (2) it fits Paul's logical progression of thought, (3) it parallels Paul's teachings elsewhere.

Paul has just spoken in verse 1 about the Ephesians having previously been dead to God. What made them dead was their sins and trespasses. That is, it was violating God's commandments, such as those found in the Torah, that made them dead. This is consistent with Paul's teachings elsewhere that breaking commandments of Torah makes one worthy of condemnation.[13] The proximity of Paul speaking of a death sentence caused by breaking the Torah fits well with interpreting Ephesians 2:15 as the abolishment of Torah's death sentence caused by written regulations.

This interpretation also fits with Paul's logical progression of thought. He is saying that Gentiles were once outsiders and estranged from God, but the death of Messiah has changed something enabling Jew and Gentile to be together in God's people. What Messiah did was cancel the death sentence of Torah for those who believe. This creates a new category of people, those who are alive in Messiah by faith, whether Jew or Gentile. God has created a new humanity, those alive in Messiah through the cancellation of the death sentence. It is these who are one new man.

Finally, the idea that Jesus' death cancels the death penalty is a Pauline idea through and through. Romans 8 says there is no condemnation and the Law of sin and death is no longer over us. Galatians 3 says that Messiah became a curse for us so that the curse of Torah (death) is removed from us. Colossians 2 says that Messiah's death cancelled the record of debt against us with its legal demands. This is why Gentiles do not have to become Jews, for salvation is not in Jewishness, but in Messiah's death whose benefit is received by faith.

One New Man

The concept of one new man formed out of Jew and Gentile is a revolutionary one. Paul calls it a mystery.[14] Paul, a highly educated Jewish student of one of history's leading rabbinical teachers, a Pharisee through and through, is saying that he now shares something in common with Gentile disciples that goes even deeper than his relationship with Israel!

Paul's thought here has implications for both churches and Messianic Jewish congregations. There must be room in every congregation for both Jews and Gentiles.

This might not seem like much of an issue, but it definitely is. In many churches, Jews are not allowed to be Jews: "Difference is bad. Jews shouldn't insist on resting on the Sabbath or avoiding the honey-baked ham at church suppers. Don't you know, Jesus died to take us away from all that?"

By contrast, many have been to Messianic Jewish synagogues and encountered the opposite problem: "Are you Jewish? Oh, you're not?" (Look of disappointment). "You can't date her, she's Jewish and you're not. You can't be a leader in this congregation — you're not Jewish!"

God, according to Paul, does not ask Jews to become Gentiles or Gentiles to become Jews. He has made one new man, Jew and Gentile together: "For through him we both have access in one Spirit to the Father."[15]

Ephesians 2:15 fits beautifully into the Jewish life and thought of Paul. Paul's passion was always for the cross, the cross of Jesus that cancels our death sentence and creates one new man, Jew and Gentile.

Discussion Questions

• What were some misunderstandings and misuses of the Law by Jews in Paul's day?

• How does Paul's use of a Torah commandment in Ephesians 6:1-3 argue against a common interpretation of Ephesians 2:15?

• What is the major issue Paul addresses in Ephesians?

• What did Aristeas say about the Torah and Jewish-Gentile relations?

• What does the Torah say about Jewish-Gentile relations?

• What is the problem with saying that the moral Laws are valid and the ceremonial Laws abolished?

• What is the problem with saying that the cross abolished commandments from the Torah separating Jews and Gentiles?

• How did abolishing the death sentence of Torah bring Jews and Gentiles together in the congregation?

• What is the one new man?

• What are implications of one new man for churches? Messianic congregations?

Chapter 10
Paul's Kingdom Thought

The pastor's conference was packed. In some sessions there wasn't enough room for all the participants. I just couldn't wait to get to the bookstore.

I knew this particular conference had a certain theological slant. I should have known that slant would not include support for Israel. I should have known the tendency would be towards replacement theology, otherwise known as supercessionism.

Supercessionism is simply the idea that God has finished, or mostly finished, his work with and through Israel. The church has replaced Israel in God's plan. Thus the promises God made to Israel are no longer for Israel.

Even though I should have known that the conference would be slanted as it was, I was not emotionally prepared for what I saw in the bookstore. What I saw was Israel left out. For example, while there was a book on Messianic Judaism, the book was against the whole idea. It vehemently opposed the idea of Jews remaining Jews in practice after coming to faith.

Then I saw a book about the land of Israel, only this book was written by an author who believes Christians should not support Israel. In fact, he believes the Palestinians should get Christian support. If you only carry one book about the land of Israel in a theological bookstore, why carry one by someone who does not support Israel the people?

Finally, I saw a table of books on the end times. Sure enough, all the books were either amillennial or postmillennial. Amillennialists believe there will not be a literal 1,000 year reign of Jesus on earth and that we are already figuratively in his reign from his throne on heaven. Postmillennialists believe the church will bring the kingdom by thoroughly Christianizing the world for 1,000 years before Jesus returns.

I wanted to see premillennial books, but there were none. Only pre-millennialism, the idea that Jesus will come first and rule the earth for 1,000 years, takes seriously God's promises to Israel through Moses and the prophets.

Clearly something is wrong when major segments of the Christian world believe God changed his mind about Israel. All is not well when Israel, one of the largest subjects in the whole Bible, is thought of as an embarrassing preface to God's true revelation in the New Testament.

I spoke with the manager of the conference bookstore, expressing my disappointment that Israel was being left out. He said, "You're right to notice that we have a theological slant. Our bookstore doesn't carry pre-millennial or pro-Israel books."

I couldn't help it. I had to reply. So I said, "Are you ever going to be surprised when you are resurrected and find yourself in Israel worshipping Jesus at the temple in Jerusalem!"

The Promises of the Prophets

Paul knew and read prophets like Isaiah and Ezekiel from the time he was a child. Unlike many modern church leaders, Paul was steeped in the Hebrew Bible.

Paul well knew the myriad of prophecies that Israel would in the future be restored. Israel would be cast out of the land, be brought back at first without faith, then be renewed and thoroughly changed. The last days would see Israel at last wholly in love with God and completely trusting in Messiah.[1]

Three promises in particular I believe were formative for Paul. Three promises especially explain Paul's kingdom thought, which shows up throughout his writings.

First, Moses had promised, "And the Lord your God will circumcise your heart and the heart of your offspring, so that you will love the Lord your God with all your heart and with all your soul."[2] The context of the promise is the last days, after Israel has been cast out of the land. God will bring Israel back and fundamentally change them. Their hearts will ever after be fully his.

Second, Jeremiah said, "This is the covenant that I will make with the house of Israel after those days, declares the Lord: I will put my Law within them, and I will write it on their hearts."[3] Here is another promise about the heart. God said he would circumcise Israel's heart in the Deuteronomy promise. Here he says he will write the Torah on their hearts, in other words cause them to fully obey the Torah.

Third, Ezekiel said, "And I will give you a new heart, and a new spirit I will put within you. And I will remove the heart of stone from your flesh and give you a heart of flesh. And I will put my Spirit within you, and cause you to walk in my statutes and be careful to obey my rules."[4] Again, the heart of Israel is changed. Very specifically Ezekiel notes that the heart change of Israel will lead to complete obedience to the Torah of Moses, right down to statutes and rules.

What Paul realized, and it was always at the center of his thought about salvation, is that righteousness is a gift from God. Righteousness does not come from within us, but from God alone. Ultimately God will be the one who makes us righteous. Perfect righteousness, a circumcised, inscribed, softened heart, will be given to Israel in the last days.

Waiting Rather Than Working For the Kingdom

Prior to meeting Jesus on the road to Damascus, Paul was working for the coming of God's kingdom. As described earlier, Paul's involvement with militant Pharisees included a movement to bring the kingdom by purifying Israel and jump-starting a Torah revival.

When Paul met Jesus on the road to Damascus, he realized something: God is bringing the kingdom himself without our help. The one executed for blasphemy was no blasphemer, but the very Messiah he said he was. The resurrection had already begun in Jesus.

Yet Paul knew the kingdom was not fully arrived. The rest of Israel was not resurrected. Israel was not yet restored. The kingdom had begun to dawn but had not fully risen. The kingdom was now and not yet.

Paul knew now that we are to be waiting for the kingdom, not working for it to come.[5] He knew that righteousness cannot be earned, but can only be received. This radically impacted his thought, not only turning him to Jesus but also away from a man-centered approach to the kingdom.

Gentiles and the Kingdom

Paul was in for another revelation in his meeting with Jesus on the Syrian road. God's plans to restore the world and bring the kingdom would include Gentiles.

Paul's realization of this fact began in Jesus' words to him. The Acts 9 account does not specifically include Paul's call to the Gentiles[6] but a fuller account in Acts 22 does. Jesus said to Paul, "Go, for I will send you far away to the Gentiles."[7] That Paul's calling was specifically to Gentiles is evident in numerous passages such as Romans 11:13.

Paul realized that the wonderful promise of the new heart, God's Spirit living within, and of a righteousness from God, was not just for Israel, but also for Gentiles. And God did not mean Gentiles could become Jews and share the blessing. God meant Gentiles, as Gentiles, would have a place in his kingdom along with Jews.

The Revealing of the Sons of God

Glorious kingdom thought occurs throughout Paul's writings. Many of these ideas are missed by the casual reader and few sermons and books really address them.

One such gem that is easily missed is in Romans 8:19. Speaking of the relationship of the believer and the Holy Spirit, Paul thinks ahead to future glory when he says, "For the creation waits with eager longing for the revealing of the sons of God."

Paul's meaning is simple. First, creation is not what it should be ever since the fall in Genesis 3. Creation is personified here, as if the world itself has emotions. The world is tired of being fallen and cannot wait to be redeemed when God perfects the world.

What is one of the great stages of that restoration that the world waits for? Creation waits to see at last the glory of the sons of God (and daughters, I'm sure Paul meant to say.)

We are the sons of God of whom Paul is speaking. With the coming of the days of Messiah, the kingdom of God fully revealed, we will also be revealed in all our glory. We will be perfect and made in the image of Jesus, without sin or blemish of any kind.

New Creations

Perhaps the best known statement of changed men and women in the kingdom is least understood. Many people memorize a powerful verse, 2 Corinthians 5:17, without understanding the full meaning.

Paul says, "Therefore, if anyone is in Christ, he is a new creation. The old has passed away; behold, the new has come." This puzzles many who quickly realize that sin has not left the building and we are not, in fact, free from its power.

Paul is saying something so simple it is a shame to miss it. Paul has in mind the whole idea of our glorification, that one day we will be made perfect like Messiah. We will have no sin and we will be immortal. Paul's point is glorious: God already regards us as the perfect people we will be, not as the struggling saints we currently are!

Remember, what Paul knew from Moses and the prophets and realized with freshness when he saw the risen Jesus is that righteousness comes from God. Self-improvement will not lead to the kind of righteousness God will give us: perfection.

Messiah already set us free from the penalty of sin, as Paul declares numerous times.[8] The Holy Spirit is daily growing us out of the power of sin.[9] One day, the Spirit will even free us from the presence of sin.[10]

God regards us the same way parents sometimes look at their children. When they are little, parents may see the runny noses, the food stains, and the undeveloped features of the child. Yet no parent ultimately imagines their child that way.

A proud parent imagines graduation day, wedding day, and the birth of grandchildren. A parent knows that their child is not yet what he or she will be. We regard them as adults in a way while they are still children. So God pictures us as grown up in him, perfect, blameless, new creations.

And for God such imagining is not difficult. Not bound by time, the past, present, and future perhaps coexist for him. That means God already knows us as our future selves. And in the expanse of forever, this little time where we are children, soiled and unready, is extremely brief.

Moses, the Prophets, and New Creations

Paul's thought about our glorification is a line from Moses, to Jeremiah, to Ezekiel, to Jesus. True righteousness comes from God and not from ourselves. God will circumcise the heart. God will write his Torah on the heart. God will give new hearts ready to obey his statutes and rules.

By contrast, some other Jewish thinkers of Paul's day sought to establish their own righteousness. It was not so much a matter of being accepted by God for their goodness as the nation being saved from Rome by Torah faithfulness.

For many of the Pharisees, those who followed Hillel, the issue was building a fence around the Torah. They sought to bring Israel's obedience into line by making Laws stricter than God's. That way, people were even less likely to break God's Law.

For others, those who followed Shammai, there was an added emphasis on militancy. Be prepared to overthrow Rome. Purify the land of heretics. When we are pure enough, God will save.

For the Essenes, the way of salvation lay in radical separation. Move out to the desert. Wash twice a day in the ritual bath. Eat Messianic meals with the community. Avoid interaction with the godless masses. God will save those who separate themselves and join the only community of the saved.

For the Sadducees, Israel's salvation would be in keeping the temple ritual intact. Keep the daily burnt offerings uninterrupted. Avoid contamination coming into the temple. Even if Rome's armies are besieging you, remain at the temple and God will even save you from the flames.

In some ways, this was a subtle error. It is true that God desires obedience to his commandments, but only for the right reasons. To obey with an agenda, to obey and make extra rules to get God's attention, is as bad as not obeying.

Paul saw it all and knew the good news of Messiah disproved the whole notion of self-attained righteousness. Jesus was risen. The kingdom was begun. God would circumcise, inscribe, and remake hearts. God would give righteousness or there would be no righteousness at all. And for those to whom God was giving righteousness, the kingdom's benefits were already accruing.

Discussion Questions

• What is premillennialism? Amillennialism? Postmillennialism?

• What is supercessionism?

• What similar foretellings do Moses, Jeremiah, and Ezekiel make about the heart?

• What do these foretellings have to do with the kingdom?

• What do these foretellings say about the source of righteousness?

• What did the revelation of the risen Jesus tell Paul about the kingdom?

• How did Paul know about Gentiles in the kingdom?

• What does Paul mean that Creation eagerly awaits the revealing of the sons and daughters of God?

• What does it mean that we are new creations?

• How did Pharisees, Essenes, and Sadducees miss God's righteousness?

Chapter 11
Paul's Message in a Nutshell

Paul's life and message have been tragically misunderstood both in Judaism and Christianity. A common line in university religion classes is that Jesus came to teach a simple Judaism centered on love and Paul complicated matters by withdrawing Christianity from its Jewish roots. A common line in popular preaching is that Paul preached freedom from the Law to make way for grace.

Paul never envisioned a church that would despise Israel. The anti-Jewish preaching of Chrysostrom, the anti-Jewish rhetoric of the church fathers, the Crusades, Inquisition, Pogroms, and Ghettos would leave Paul enraged, not proud.

Should Paul attend a church service in an average town on an average Sunday morning and hear his message distorted, could he possibly be pleased? In realizing Gentiles' freedom from Jewish conversion, would Paul have ever envisioned a church that imagines it has replaced Israel? A church that has renamed the day of Messiah's resurrection Easter after a pagan goddess?[1]

Thanks be to God that the church did not distort Paul's primary message: God's righteousness comes to us as a gift through Jesus. Self-attained righteousness is a myth and an affront to God who has always promised to give righteousness to those who believe.

Of course, the church has at times and in places distorted even that message. Much of the modern Protestant reading of Paul has come through the Reformation. The church was selling salvation from the bank of the good deeds of the saints. The Reformers stood up and declared that salvation is by faith alone.

Isn't it time for another aspect of reformation? If the truth of God's righteousness given freely has returned, why not the truth of Israel's place in God's plan? Why not the truth of the kingdom promised by Jewish prophets?

Paul's Jewish Life

Before knowing Jesus, Paul was a Pharisee trying to speed the kingdom by purifying Israel. After knowing Jesus, Paul was a Pharisee trying to save Israel by telling them of God's kingdom already begun.

For moderns, it seems contradictory to say at once that Paul was Jewish or a Pharisee and at the same time a Christian (in the modern parlance of a follower of Messiah). Paul was a Messianic Jew, a Christian Pharisee, if you will. He saw no conflict between Moses and Jesus because there is no conflict between Moses and Jesus.

For moderns, it is all but impossible to imagine Paul, the favorite revealer of Christianity, in the temple offering sacrifices after knowing Jesus. The idea that Judaism and the Law of Moses are in opposition to Christianity is so ingrained as to be axiomatic.

This tempts well-meaning interpreters to explain the paradox of the book of Acts. Paul did those Jewish things because he wanted to win his Jewish brothers to the faith. Didn't Paul say, "To the Jews I became as a Jew, in order to win Jews. To those under the Law I became as one under the Law (though not being myself under the Law) that I might win those under the Law"?[2]

Thus, Paul kept the Torah and traditions of Judaism post-Jesus merely to make Christianity more palatable to Torah-observant Jews. The idea is absurd.

First, Paul would himself be a hypocrite. Knowing, allegedly, that the Torah is obsolete and has nothing to do with Jesus, he would practice it nonetheless to win Jews? If this is what Paul meant in 1 Corinthians 9:20, then perhaps in vs.21 ("to those outside the Law I became as one outside the Law") Paul meant he engaged in drunkenness and other sins to make Christianity more palatable to Gentiles!

Second, Paul was never one to compromise on any point of truth for the sake of peace. He opposed Peter, Barnabas, and the whole group of Messianic Jews to their face in Antioch when they stopped sharing the table with Gentiles.[3] Paul would never feign interest in Judaism disingenuously to better proselytize Jews.

Paul's Jewish life can only be understood in one way: the Torah and faith in Jesus are intertwined, interdependent, and completely compatible. Paul, the Jesus-believing Pharisee, was no paradox or contradiction, but the model for any Jesus-believing Jew today.

The Kingdom of God's Righteousness

The heart of Paul's message is that in Jesus the kingdom has broken into our age. In Jesus, God's righteousness is being made available to us.

This is no small admission for a man whose early career was distinguished by his attempts to bring God's kingdom by Pharisaic militancy. What the house of Shammai and people like Paul could never accomplish by legislating and purging, God had done by bringing his Son.

In Romans, Paul makes the message of God's righteousness clear, showing the need for both Jews and Gentiles to receive it freely. In Galatians, Paul stands against an attempt to manufacture righteousness through conversion. Nothing less than God's righteousness will do. In Ephesians, Paul clarifies the radical result of God's righteousness poured out on Jew and Gentile. There is now a third community of humankind, one new man consisting of Jew and Gentile sharing one faith, one Lord, one Baptism.

When Jesus rose, the kingdom had begun to dawn on this age. Jesus' resurrection was a precursor to our own in the age when the kingdom fully arrives.

In the kingdom, Torah and prophets agree, God's righteousness is freely given. Hearts are circumcised. Torah is written on the heart. New hearts are given.

But God's righteousness freely given, to Jews and Gentiles, does not negate Israel or the Torah. Why would the coming of a kingdom announced through Jewish prophets mean the cessation of Jewish life and revelation?

Paul on Torah

Far from being an impediment to God's righteousness, the Torah is a revelation of God's righteousness. When God gives his righteousness freely to Jew and Gentile, Torah does not go away. It is the same righteousness.

The Torah is spiritual, but we are slaves sold under sin.[5] There is nothing fleshy about the Torah. It is true that Paul speaks of Galatians relying on circumcision for conversion as returning to the elementary principles of the world.[6] But it is misusing the Torah that is fleshy, not the Torah itself.

The flesh is not the Torah, but our rebellion against God which is systemic. Torah is righteous, but our flesh resists the Torah and does what is evil.[7] Jesus did not come to set us free from the Torah,[8] but to set us free from the curse of the Torah which is death for disobedience.[9]

Therefore we are free from the Law of sin and death, the Torah's condemning function.[10] There is no more condemnation.[11] Yet this does not set us free from the Torah's truth.

The allegory of the guardian or pedagogue is a perfect description of the role of the Torah.[12] Many interpreters feel Paul's allegory means the Torah is now obsolete since we are grown up. Yet in reality this is a poor interpretation of the allegory. What we have outgrown is not the truth of the pedagogue's instruction in manners, but the discipline of the pedagogue when we act against those manners. In other words, we've outgrown the Torah's penalty but not the Torah's truth.

Just as Torah as commandment and truth has not been displaced by the advancing kingdom, neither has Israel. Paul's take on Israel is equally important to realizing the implications of God's righteousness freely given.

Paul on Israel

Israel was both a blessing and a problem for the Gentiles coming to God in Paul's day. They were a blessing as forebears and believers in the one God of the Bible. They were a problem in their rejection of a savior promised in the same scriptures.

Paul's teaching on Israel explained the seeming paradox wonderfully. Israel had never been a community of believers. Nor had all the descendants of Abraham always inherited the promise. Just as Ishmael and Esau missed out, so too many in Israel would miss out.[13] Not all in Israel entered the promised land, but only those who believed.[14] Israel's unbelief should not be a surprise, for the Hebrew Bible is filled with the unbelief of Israel.

Yet Gentiles should not get from this truth the idea that Israel is rejected by God.[15] In fact, our faith can be described as a Jewish olive tree.[16] The Gentile branches grafted in should not despise the Jewish root.[17] Those who think they stand should be careful lest they fall,[18] and grafted in branches could be cut off.[19]

The fact is, Israel is blessed because of the patriarchs[20] and Israel's promises are still valid.[21] The day is certainly coming when all Israel will be saved.[22] In fact, unbelieving Israel, though causing the believers trouble, should not be looked down upon. They should be seen as weak,[23] thinking that Torah obedience is what places one within God's covenant when the strong know that God's covenant is given freely. By the certainty of our belief we should not destroy the one for whom Messiah died.[24] We should not let our dogmatic correctness push Israel away. We should not become ridiculers and tormentors of Israel, but lovers and rescuers.

In the meantime, there is a remnant of believing Israel[25] and a majority of rejecting Israel. Rejecting Israel in many ways has become an enemy of the gospel.[26] Yet Paul quotes the prophets regarding Israel's glorious future.[27] As Isaiah 59 and Jeremiah 31 affirm, in the days of Messiah, Israel will be turned away from ungodliness and be saved. What the followers of Jesus must do in the meantime is respect the Jewish root and proclaim the message.[28]

While understanding Israel in this way, it is also vital to understand the Gentiles in Paul's thought. The Torah and Israel certainly fit into Paul's realization that the kingdom had dawned in Jesus. There were already promises Israel waited to see fulfilled in those days. What about Gentiles?

Paul on Gentiles

Rather than Israel's place in the covenant being controversial, it is really the place of non-Israel that should be controversial. How can Gentiles be saved by a Jewish Messiah through promises made to the Jews?

Some people think this is where Paul was really an innovator. The truth is, Paul had plenty of precedent for his teachings on Gentiles: precedents from the Torah, prophets, and Jesus.

First, the place of the Gentiles in this dawning kingdom of Messiah was evident in Jesus' call. Jesus himself had called Paul to preach the good news to the Gentiles.[29] Jesus did not merely call Paul to Gentile converts, who were practically regarded as Jews. Nor was the call limited to Gentile God-fearers who were already very Jewish in outlook. The call was to Gentiles as Gentiles.

Second, Paul was very aware of God's plan for the nations, the Gentiles, in the Torah itself. Paul chose one of the best-known and simplest passages from the Torah to explain God's plan. The place of the Gentiles, Paul declared, was revealed in the promise to Abraham.[30]

One way of showing the place of the Gentiles is to note the surprising truth that Abraham himself was a Gentile. Abraham was uncircumcised when he received the promise, indicating that he was not only the father of the Jews but also of all who believe even if not circumcised.[31] Abraham, while uncircumcised, received a promise of great blessing which is still being fulfilled. God's promise does not depend on circumcision and therefore applies to the circumcised and uncircumcised, Jew and Gentile.

Another way to show this is through the wording of one of the promises. God promised to make Abraham a blessing to all nations.[32] Paul called this the gospel preached in advance to Gentiles.[33] God had intended all along for his promises to go through Abraham to the Gentiles. The Torah itself said so.

Third, Paul was aware that the prophets foretold the salvation of Gentiles as Gentiles. Hosea spoke of a time when God would say "my people" to those who were not his people.[34] Paul's comment on the verse is that God has called from both Jew and Gentile a people for his glory.[35] Paul stood by in agreement when James declared the same truth from Amos.[36] James saw the truth in Amos's statement that in the last days Gentiles will be called by God's name.[37]

The Gentiles, Paul would say, had once been alienated from the commonwealth of Israel, but in the dawning of the kingdom had been brought near.[38] The death penalty of the Torah had been removed for Jew and Gentile, creating a new community of redeemed Jews and Gentiles.[39] God had made Jew and Gentile one in the congregation of Messiah.

The key to understanding Paul's thought, however, is realizing that Gentiles did not have to become Jews. The Torah teaches, and Paul assumed, that some commandments are specific to Israel, to set Israel apart as a chosen nation. Paul didn't expect that Gentiles would keep the Sabbath for example, which was a sign between Israel and God.[40] Paul spoke of certain weak people, non-believing Jews, who were scandalized by Gentiles not observing the Sabbath.[41] Paul agreed with the Jerusalem Council not to circumcise Gentiles or make them obey Jewish distinctives.[42]

This was why Paul was dismayed to find Gentiles observing days, months, seasons, and years, meaning Jewish observances.[43] They were abandoning their Greco-Roman calendars for the Jewish calendar out of compulsion. Paul had no problem with a Gentile honoring those days in honor of the Lord.[44] The problem was making Gentiles feel second-class, as if the cross had not made them clean already.

As for Gentiles and the Torah, Paul expected them to obey it. He told them on several occasions to obey commandments from the Torah.[45] The issue was not an obsolete Torah, but freedom from Torah's penalty and freedom from conversion to Jewishness.

Conclusion

I wish all along I had known Paul the Pharisee. I used to avoid books like Leviticus. Since I believed that the Torah had only historical value, I never felt compelled to understand it.

A conversation with a friend illustrates the tragedy of missing Paul's point. My friend loves studying and teaching the Hebrew background of the New Testament. People pay to hear him speak about it.

I was surprised then, when he told me about his brother, who is a theologian. His brother cannot see it at all. Judaism is legalism and the Law of Moses is irrelevant.

"Does your brother believe the Bible is inspired?" I asked. He nodded. "What does he say about Jesus' teaching that the Law will never pass away?"

"He says Paul changed everything," my friend smiled sadly.

Was my friend's brother a closet liberal? Probably not, since theological liberals do not affirm the inerrancy of the Bible.

I have encountered the same attitude numerous times in the church. For a time my wife and I belonged to a contemporary church. Many aspects of the church were wonderful.

Yet, in spite of the fact that neither my wife nor I grew up Jewish, the holidays were always a problem. Passover would come and the church saw no purpose in celebrating or remembering it. At Yom Kippur, year after year, the opportunity was passed to preach on atonement.

Sermons were never preached from Deuteronomy. Israel was never the subject of a sermon. Paul's writings were almost the exclusive source of sermon texts. And Paul was misunderstood, misrepresented, because something other than the Word of God fed those sermons.[46]

One day, my wife admitted she was not satisfied. "I can't read about all these things in the Bible and worship with people who don't care about them."

The Word of God is a building. The books of Moses are the foundation. The history and prophets and writings build on that foundation, adding little that is new, but applying the truths of Torah in multiple ways.

The New Testament was not a new building built on the rubble of the Hebrew Bible. Rather, the New Testament is the upper third of the house, the highest floors. And Paul is not the demolisher of the lower floors, but an expert builder who added his work on top of them.

Paul read and studied the whole Bible, which did not yet include the

New Testament. He hung out in Moses and Isaiah, and could quote them freely. It was Paul who said, "All Scripture is breathed out by God."[47] Far from making new truth or taking the faith away from the old truths, Paul revered the Hebrew Bible and saw his own teaching as interpretation rather than innovation.

Appendices

Appendix A: Frequent Questions and Objections About Torah-Observance

1. Isn't grace opposed to Law-keeping?

Grace is the English translation of a rather common Greek word, *charis* (kar-ees), with two basic meanings: (1) charm, (2) favor. In the New Testament, the word is most often used for favor, and even more specifically for undeserved favor, as in God favoring us though we don't deserve it.

The New Testament doctrine of grace is no more opposed to Law-keeping than it is to righteousness. Consider the following obvious falsehood: "We are under grace, therefore lie, cheat, and steal as you please."

Just as morals and righteousness are not opposed to grace, neither is any precept of the Torah. If a Messianic Jew, or a Gentile who wishes to do so, avoids eating pork, he or she is not denying grace, but keeping a commandment.

It is not against grace to say that keeping a Torah commandment is required. It does not contradict grace to say, "You're Jewish and God expects you to observe the Sabbath." This is analogous to saying to a Gentile disciple, "You follow Jesus and he expects you to stop lying."

Yet it is wrong to say that God will not accept you unless you keep the Torah. That would be analogous to saying, "You cannot be accepted by God because of your habit of lying." We know that disciples still sin and yet God accepts them in Messiah as his people.

2. Didn't Jesus declare all foods clean?

Sadly, this myth is perpetuated by English Bible translations. The verse in question is Mark 7:19. Many read this verse as part of a discussion about Jewish food Laws. The New International Version says, "For it doesn't go into his heart but into his stomach and then out of his body. (In saying this, Jesus declared all foods 'clean')." The common interpretation is that Jesus was overturning God's Law in Leviticus 11 and saying that all kinds of food are clean.

First of all, even before considering the faulty translation of Mark 7:19, are two simple reasons not to take the common interpretation: (1) this discussion is about Jewish hand-washing Laws rather than dietary Laws and (2) Jesus would never overturn a Law of God, and he said so clearly in Matthew 5:17.

The King James and older English versions got this right, but modern versions distort the passage. In Mark 7:19, the King James says, "Because it entereth not into his heart, but into the belly, and goeth out into the draught, purging all meats?" Where the NIV says, "(In saying this, Jesus declared all foods 'clean')," the KJV has "purging all meats."

The King James and other ancient English translations are correct. The Greek text of Mark 7:19 does not have the words "Jesus declared," but merely a participial phrase, "cleansing all foods." The modern translators have been doing some interpretation without disclosure in their renderings. They are taking the participial phrase to mean, "Thereby Jesus was cleansing all foods, i.e. saying that all kinds of food are clean in contrast to the Torah's prohibitions."

The King James has not only left the phrase as it is, but suggests another interpretation. At issue in Mark is not the inherent purity or impurity of such meats as pork. The issue is ritual handwashing. Some in Israel poured water over their hands ceremoniously before eating to ritually purify their hands, which may have touched Gentiles who may have touched unclean things. Otherwise, it was believed, that uncleanness on the hands would pass to the food and make you unclean. Jesus' point in Mark 7:19 is simple: uncleanness is real, but it cannot be passed on by eating food. Food goes into the stomach and is passed into the latrine, purging everything from inside you. No impurity remains within you. This is a far cry from Jesus overturning the Law and promoting the pork council!

3. Didn't Peter see a vision telling him to eat non-kosher meat?

The text in question is Acts 10:9-23. Peter received a vision, not the actual objects, of a sheet containing numerous animals, birds, and creeping things. Was this vision about God repealing his Laws from Leviticus 11 and making all kinds of meat clean?

First, if you wish to interpret this vision as permission to eat anything, be prepared to eat them all: including creeping things and all the birds of the air. Peter didn't see a sheet with a pork frankfurter (a pig in the blanket!) or a juicy honey-baked ham. He saw animals including rats, spiders, bats, and worms!

Second, note that Peter did not eat anything. It was a vision.

Third, note that the vision had nothing to do with dietary Laws. It had to do with Gentiles being clean and acceptable to God. God made an analogy between unclean animals and Gentiles. The point of the analogy is that Gentiles are not impure like some kinds of meat.

Fourth, note that Cornelius was a God-fearer. This probably meant that he himself avoided unclean meat. Certainly, as one who was frequently with Jews, he would not have served unclean meat when Peter visited.

4. Shouldn't everyone, Jew and Gentile, keep the Law the same?

The Torah has many commandments. The rabbis count 613, but there is room to debate over how to number them. By the way, some say the New Testament has over 1,000 commandments.

All of the commandments of the Torah are relevant, but not all apply to everyone and not all can even still be applied to anyone.

For example, God commanded the priests not to marry a divorced woman in Leviticus 21:7. Does this verse mean that no one should marry a divorced woman? Of course not, it says a priest should not. (Imagine someone using 1 Peter 2:9 to make a case that no follower of Jesus should marry a divorced woman!).

It is possible that some commandments of the Torah were strictly for Israel. The most obvious and agreed-upon example is circumcision. God commanded descendants of Abraham, Isaac, and Jacob to be circumcised, which signified belonging to the covenant. In the New Testament, Paul understood clearly that Gentiles need not be circumcised (Galatians 2:3). Yet Paul had Timothy circumcised in Acts 16:3.

Other commandments from the Torah that seem Israel-specific include: Sabbath observance, wearing fringes as commanded in Numbers 15:38, dietary Laws (note that accidentally killed meat could be sold to Gentiles as per Deuteronomy 14:21), and obligatory attendance at the temple for holy days.

The two commandments from this list most debated are Sabbath and dietary Laws. Many people believe the Sabbath is a commandment required of everyone. After all, it is in the ten commandments.

Yet, God is not on record as ever commanding Sabbath observance until two weeks after the people left Egypt. He didn't even tell the Israelites until the eve of the Sabbath as they gathered manna in Exodus 16:23. Note that in Genesis 2:2 and 3, God hallowed the Sabbath but he did not command observance. God called the Sabbath a sign between him and Israel forever in Exodus 31:13. This probably means the Sabbath was a way Israel lived differently from the nations, a special calling for God's Chosen People.

Also, the dietary Laws are another example of God calling Israel to be different from the nations. Deuteronomy 14:21 is a hint that dietary Laws were never meant to be universal. Israelites could sell meat found dead to sojourners and foreigners even though it was forbidden for Israel to eat them.

The New Testament confirms that Sabbath and dietary Law were not required for Gentile disciples. First, in the letter from the Jerusalem Council, Sabbath and dietary Laws (except eating blood and idol-meat) were not mentioned. Second, Paul in Galatians 4:10 insists that days, months, seasons, and years are not required of Gentiles. He says in Romans 14:5, "One person esteems one day as better than another, while another esteems all days alike." The context is clearly Jewish-Gentile relations and it seems forced to say Paul was not addressing the Sabbath.

5. Would God expect different requirements from different groups, such as you are suggesting about Jews and Gentiles?

Differences do not mean inequality. In Israel, priests and Levites were not higher than other Israelites, yet in many ways requirements differed. Could a member of the tribe of Asher complain to God, "You're not treating me equally since I cannot serve as a Levite"?

Nearly everyone admits that God does not require circumcision of Gentiles, which is a difference. This is not inequality but distinction.

Some people object based on Galatians 3:28, which says there is neither Jew nor Greek. The meaning clearly is not that there are no differences between Jew and Greek, but that God accepts all equally. The verse also says there is neither male nor female, yet there are different requirements for women than men in both the Torah and the New Testament. Also, I've yet to see a person use Galatians 3:28 as permission for women to use the men's restroom!

Other distinctions in scripture include teachers versus non-teachers, deacons and elders versus non-leadership in the congregation. Different roles should be expected in the community without the charge of inequality.

6. Does this mean Jews are on a higher level?

As God's elect people, Israel is still being used in a unique way by God. Nor has Israel received yet all that has been promised to the nation. God will not change his promise or fail to fulfill it, as Paul says in Romans 11:29. Unredeemed Israel in the present time receives a certain grace in national affairs from God as well as a certain judgment specific to Israel.

Redeemed Israel in the Messianic Age will own the land long ago promised to Abraham.

Yet, for all these distinctions, and even the idea that Jews are required to keep some commandments not required of Gentiles, there is no issue of favoritism. Galatians 3:28 says it plainly: God does not differentiate in blessing between Jews and Gentiles.

7. Does this mean Gentiles cannot or should not keep all of Torah and/or live as Jews?

There are reasons why some Gentiles will choose to keep some or all of the Torah commandments specific to Israel.

First, a common reason many Gentiles restrict their meat to the clean meats listed in Leviticus 11 is a belief that clean meat is healthier. This is almost certainly not the reason God gave the Laws in Leviticus 11. Nor is it likely that all unclean meats are less healthy than clean ones. Yet health or a desire to eat God's diet is nonetheless a possible and popular reason for eating only clean meats.

Second, some Gentiles may feel a special calling to live fully as Jews. Though it is not required, they may have their sons circumcised on the eighth day, rest on the Sabbath, and keep dietary Laws. The choice of a foreigner to join with Israel in this way has a precedent in the Torah itself.

In Exodus 12:48, God gives Israel the case of a foreigner who desires to eat the sacred Passover sacrifice like the Israelite families. The stranger may do so if he and his sons are circumcised and he shall be as a native Israelite. No conversion ceremony besides circumcision is mentioned. Some object that this could only apply to a Gentile living in the land, but there is not sufficient reason to assume a Gentile living outside the land might make the same choice.

Finally, some Gentiles will want to keep some of all of the Laws specific to Israel for a variety of reasons. A common example would be the celebration of Israel's holy days. Temple attendance is not an issue in our time, but observances such as fasting on Yom Kippur, eating only unleavened bread during the week of Passover, and living in booths during the Feast of Tabernacles (Booths) are common. There are a variety of reasons Gentiles may wish to do this: to prepare for the Messianic Age when all will keep the holy days (see Zech. 14:16), to identify with Israel and Jewish friends, or simply to experience and live out Biblical customs as a form of worship.

8. Are you saying that evangelical/Protestant churches are unbiblical?

It is not unbiblical for Gentile disciples to work on the Sabbath or eat pork and other unclean meat. Paul says not to judge the Lord's servant over such issues in Romans 14:4.

What is unbiblical is anti-Jewish teaching. All too often, teachers in churches make the mistake of assuming that the church (the congregation of Messiah) has replaced Israel as God's Chosen People. Paul wrote clearly against this idea in passages such as Romans 11. Also, teaching that the Law of God, the Torah, is somehow unspiritual or misguided not only demeans Israel, but also God who gave the Law.

An extreme example is worth mentioning. Adam Clarke is a commentator from a previous century, but his notes on the Bible are a common resource for Christian leaders. Commenting on Hebrews 7:18, he says:

> The Jews, who still cleave to it, are a proof that it is both weak
> and unprofitable; for there is not a more miserable, distressed,
> and profligate class of men on the face of the earth.

In other words, the Torah of God is proven to be useless because one only has to look at Jews to see what a profligate (sinful, immoral, lustful) group they are. This is unbiblical (as well as anti-Semitic) and in less extreme form is taught in far too many pulpits and classrooms.

9. Are you calling for Jews and Gentiles to separate into different congregations?

In many cases today it is a good idea for Jewish disciples to separate into Messianic Congregations. Yet it is not inherently necessary.

On the one hand, the Biblical ideal is Jew and Gentile together. On the other hand, in a climate where Jewishness is not valued, where a Jewish disciple will be pressured and encouraged to abandon Jewish distinctives, separation may be warranted.

Let it be said that Messianic Congregations are primarily Gentile in membership, so Jew and Gentile are together there. Let it also be said that when church leaders understand and make room for Jews to be Jews, then there is not a necessity for separate Jewish congregations.

Separation based on preferences and ethnic identities is not wrong. Division based on the same, however, is wrong.

Thus, while Messianic Congregations and evangelical churches may be separate in many cases, there should not be division between them.

Jews and Gentiles are one in the congregation of Messiah. There should be cooperation and mutual trust. There should be participation together in God's work around the world without division.

This cooperation is not commonly seen in the present Christian world. Blame is on both sides, Messianic Congregations who distrust and malign churches and churches who reciprocate. Would that we would realize the truth of Paul's statement in Ephesians that we are now one new man, Jew and Gentile!

Appendix B: What Would Torah-Observance Look Like?

1. It would look different for Jews and Gentiles.

Some protest that it is unjust for God to have different standards for different groups, but God has always worked this way.

For example, a priest could not marry a divorced woman (Leviticus 21:7) but other Israelites could. Priests were held to a different standard.

In the New Testament, James mentions that teachers are judged according to a higher standard (James 3:1).

God also gave breaks to pagans that he would never have given to Israelites. For example, Jonah said to Ninevah, "Yet forty days, and Nineveh shall be overthrown!" (Jonah 3:4). The people reasoned that God might relent if they showed public repentance. They put sackcloth on their bodies and ashes on their heads. God relented from destruction.

Now the Ninevites, as we know from subsequent history, did not put their faith in God. They did not give up pagan ways. In fact, Assyria, with Ninevah as capital, still attacked and destroyed Israel a generation later.

God would not have given Israel such a break for mere temporary repentance. The fact is, Ninevah was judged according to a lower standard.

As discussed in Chapter 4, the Jerusalem Council made it clear that Gentiles have a different relationship with the Torah than Jews. When the New Testament hints at specifics, such as in Galatians 4:10 and Romans 14:1-6, the list of differences tends to include Sabbath, holy days, and dietary Laws.

We should know from Torah itself that these Laws were given as sign commandments to Israel. The Sabbath is called a sign between Israel and God in Exodus 31:13 and is never commanded specifically for Gentiles outside the land of Israel. The dietary Laws have to do with Israel being sanctified as a nation according to Leviticus 11:44. Furthermore, meat considered unclean because it was found dead may still be sold to Gentiles according to Deuteronomy 14:21.

In my opinion, Gentiles were also never expected to make the three-times a year pilgrimage to the sanctuary for the holy days. Clearly Gentiles need not be circumcised. Nor do Gentiles have to wear fringes on their garments (the basis of the prayer shawl) as Numbers 15:38 commands Israel.

2. Not all Torah commandments can be literally observed.

The Torah has many kinds of commandments. Some were specific to an individual, such as God commanding Abram to leave his father's house (Genesis 12:1) or commanding the Israelites to wash their garments in preparation for Mt. Sinai (Exodus 19:10).

Some commandments in the Torah changed as the situation changed. For example, the people were told in Numbers 2 how to set up their camps around the tabernacle. When they entered the land, however, this commandment was obsolete. They had assigned territories spread out over the whole land.

There is at least one other example of a change. In Leviticus 17:3-4, God commanded that anyone in Israel who wanted to eat meat had to bring the animal as a gift to the altar. Certain portions would be burned to God and the rest eaten. This would not be practical once Israel entered the land, and God changed the commandment. In Deuteronomy 12:15, God said Israel could slaughter meat in any of their towns.

There is a principle here: some of God's commandments are bound to certain situations and they do not apply if the situation no longer fits.

The most obvious example stems from the lack of a functioning temple in our day. The reason there are no sacrifices is not because Jesus fulfilled them on the cross. He didn't. Jesus actually did something much better on the cross. He gave a new kind of sacrifice that cleanses the sinner and not just the sinner's pollution of the sanctuary (see chapter 4, under the heading "Paul and His Nazirite Vow" for more explanation). There are no sacrifices because there is no temple and God's presence does not dwell in the land.

God's presence will one day return to the land of Israel, as Ezekiel saw in 43:5. In that day, as Ezekiel spells out in the surrounding chapters, there will again be sacrifices in the temple. Yet in the meantime, there are numerous commandments in the Torah that we cannot literally apply.

We cannot establish a priesthood and levitical system until the temple is rebuilt. We cannot maintain the daily, weekly, and holy day offerings. Nor can we maintain the system of clean and unclean, for uncleanness has no meaning without a holy sanctuary.

Note this is not at all the same as dividing the Law into so-called moral and ceremonial categories. God does not divide his Law that way and such thinking is based on error. We do not decide nor is it self-evident what is moral or not. Whatever God says to do is moral and not to do is immoral. God is not bound by a higher Law than himself. The issue is not labeling Laws in categories, but examining each Law and asking the question, "Given the change in situation, can this Law still be applied?"

Another major factor in commandments being inapplicable is the governmental system of Israel, a theocracy. Not only was Israel led by God through priests, prophets, and kings, but his immediate revelation was available to the court for difficult cases. God communicated with the priests through the Urim and Thummim (Exodus 28:30). God literally was the highest judge in Israel's Law system.

Thus, many of Israel's Laws pertaining to justice and retribution cannot be applied in the same way. For example, it is not possible to stone people to death without the permission of the local government. Even in modern Israel, such Laws cannot currently be applied exactly as stated in the Torah until the kingdom is fully realized and Israel is again a theocracy.

The rabbis of Jewish history and modern Orthodox Jewish rabbis recognize the same principle. By their count there are 613 commandments in the Torah. A large portion of these cannot be directly applied in our day.

3. A commandment does not have to be repeated in the New Testament to be valid and relevant.

If you understand Paul's teaching on the Torah properly, you no longer have to divide your Bible into parts. You no longer have to think of some parts as more applicable than others.

If you are a Jewish follower of Jesus, then the commandment to circumcise your sons on the eighth day applies to you. You are to rest on the Sabbath from Friday at sundown until Saturday at sundown. You are to observe whatever parts of the holy days that can be observed in a world without a temple. You are to rid your house of leaven for the days of Passover and Unleavened Bread. You are to deny yourself on Yom Kippur, as Torah says.

It does not matter that these commandments are not repeated in the New Testament. God needs only to command something once.

The only reason people look for a command to be repeated in the New Testament is if they assume the New Testament makes the Hebrew Bible obsolete. As I have endeavored to show in this book, that is an idea Paul would vehemently oppose.

If you are a Gentile, you should know from the Hebrew Bible and the New Testament that some Torah commands are not required of you. Be aware that in the Messianic Age you will keep these commandments. Isaiah mentions the Sabbath being kept in the kingdom in 66:22-23. Zechariah mentions that Gentiles will keep the Feast of Tabernacles in 14:16. Isaiah even says that some Gentiles will be chosen as priests in the kingdom temple (66:21).

In the meantime, God has not commanded you to separate yourself from pork and other meat called unclean for Israel. God has not commanded you to rest on the Sabbath or observe the Holy Days (with the possible exception of Passover at which Jesus told his disciples to remember him in 1 Corinthians 11:25).

But do not think that because you are a Gentile the Torah does not apply to you. As you read the Torah, you will find numerous commandments that do apply, even some that are not repeated in the New Testament.

Some of these commandments have to do with justice. For example, Exodus 22:14 says that if you borrow something and it is lost or destroyed you must replace it. The court system may not agree that you have this responsibility, but the Torah says so. The New Testament does not repeat this commandment, but someone who loves God and follows the scripture will obey it.

Some of the commandments are case Laws for the courts, but they still have application for us. For example, God commanded that all roofs have a railing to protect against falls (Deuteronomy 22:8). Roofs in those days were a room of the house to be walked on.

Therefore, the point of this Law is not to build a railing on a modern house, where the roof is most likely not for human habitation. The point is that you are liable for injuries caused by negligence on your property. Therefore, it is your responsibility to fence or cover a swimming pool, as an example, so you will not be guilty of a child's death. This commandment is not in the New Testament, but it applies directly when interpreted properly.

4. Torah-observance should not be legalism.

Legalism is a word often-used and rarely understood. Suppose that Tom has been convinced through study and prayer that he should avoid movies that cause sexual temptation. Tom may have in mind Jesus' command not to look lustfully at a woman. Further suppose that John invites Tom over to watch a movie excellent in many ways but with sexual overtones. When Tom refuses to watch the movie, John may use the L-word, "Don't be legalistic."

This illustration is an example of what legalism does not mean. Legalism has three primary meanings:

1. Believing that obedience and good deeds earn God's favor for salvation (i.e. works-based righteousness).
2. Making man-made rules and treating them like divinely ordained ones.
3. Trying to keep God's commandments with human power instead of Spirit power.

An example of the first kind of legalism is someone who believes that no one who gets a divorce could be a redeemed believer. The underlying assumption is that anyone who is saved has earned their place by obeying God. To sin, especially a gross sin, is to lose salvation because God only saves those who deserve it.

An example of the second kind of legalism is someone who judges others for drinking alcohol. While scripture forbids drunkenness, it does not disparage the consumption of alcohol.

An example of the third kind of legalism is someone who takes a self-help class to get better at loving other people. This error is more subtle. Paul said that since we live by the Spirit (which is to say that we have eternal life by him) we should walk by the Spirit (find in the Spirit the source of power to obey God, Galatians 5:25). It is legalism to try to be righteous by self-effort as opposed to drawing near to God and getting his help.

Keeping the commandments of the Torah should not become legalism. No one should think that Torah-keeping is necessary to earn salvation. Nor should anyone interpret Torah in such a way that they impose man-made rules on others (like the Pharisees who said that eating raw grain picked from a field was a sin on the Sabbath).

This is not to say that Torah-obedience, like all scripture obedience, is unrelated to salvation. Saved people are changed and want to obey God. Gross disobedience to God's commandments should raise a caution about someone's sincerity in their faith.

Nor is it to say that disobeying a Torah command is not wrong. It is wrong to break a commandment regardless of where the commandment is found. If a Jewish disciple fails to rest on the Sabbath, it is a sin. If a Gentile disciple fails to pay back something that was borrowed and lost, it is a sin.

It is not legalism to say that God demands obedience. We are used to this already when we say it is a sin for someone to have an extramarital affair. Just as God commanded us not to commit adultery, he also commanded us to make restitution for lost items. To break a commandment is a sin.

Some people might say, "This sounds like legalism because it sounds like a great burden to learn and keep all these commandments." Well, God told us it is not a burden to keep his commands (1 John 5:3) and that if we love him we will (John 14:15). It is a joy to learn to live in God's righteousness powered by his Spirit.

The most subtle form of legalism is when we use human means to try to obtain divine gifts. God wants to give us righteousness. If we look for righteousness in self-help we miss God's help. The Galatians wanted to achieve a higher level through a physical ceremony. What they should have done was learn everything they could from God's Word and depended on God to help them live out what they learned. That is what it means to walk by the Spirit.

If we study God's book, inspired by the Spirit, God will cause us to keep his commandments. Along with studying God's book must come a recognition of and cooperation with the Spirit's work in us. The Spirit leads us to repent of a thousand selfish acts and thoughts. The Spirit places a hunger and desire for righteousness in us that we should learn to follow.

Thus, if you borrow a neighbor's winter coat and ruin it, you will feel wrong about shirking responsibility. The Spirit will lead you to do what is right. If you have studied the scripture, in this case Exodus 22:14, you will better understand the Spirit's leading.

5. Torah commandments should be treated with the same respect and interpretive principles as New Testament commandments.
Just as is the case with the Torah, not every New Testament commandment applies to us. Some are obvious, such as when Paul commands Timothy to bring him a cloak in 2 Timothy 4:13. Others require a great deal more thought, such as when Paul commands that women be silent in the congregation (1 Corinthians 14:34).

How should this command be interpreted? Was this something for their culture and time or is it universal? What kind of speaking by a woman does Paul forbid? If a woman sees her child about to be hurt and calls out in congregation has she sinned?

With respect to Torah commandments, the same kind of interpretive questions should be asked. What was the original intent of this command? Is it universal, to a specific group, or bound to a situation or time?

Treating the Torah like the rest of the Bible should be the obvious result of our belief that the Bible is infallible, perfect, without error. Years of neglecting the Torah may make interpretation difficult at first. But the adventure of reading, growing, and learning will be worth it.

End Notes

Chapter 1: Paul — The Misunderstood Pharisee

1. Bruce, F.F. Paul: *Apostle of the Heart Set Free*. Grand Rapids: Eerdmans, 1998 (original edition 1977), p.468.
2. ibid. p.468.
3. 1 Corinthians 9:20-21.
4. Galatians 2:11-16.
5. Matthew 5:17-19.
6. 2 Timothy 3:16-17.
7. Roetzel, Calvin. "Paul in the Second Century," in *The Cambridge Companion to St. Paul*, ed. James D.G. Dunn. Cambridge: Cambridge University Press, 2003, p.229.
8. ibid. p.230.

Chapter 2: Road to Damascus

1. Acts 22:3.
2. c.f. Wright, N.T. *What St. Paul Really Said*. Grand Rapids: Eerdmans, 1997. Pp.26-29.
3. Numbers 25:7.
4. Yeshua was Jesus' Hebrew name. Jesus is an English derivation from the Greek *Iesous*.
5. Acts 5:38-39.

Chapter 3 Notes: Paul Against the Torah?

1. Romans 4:5.
2. James 2:18.
3. Romans 4:2.
4. James 2:21.
5. Antiquities 20.9.1. Maier, Paul L. *The New Complete Works of Josephus*. Grand Rapids: Kregel, 1999. p.656.
6. Acts 21:18-20.
7. Galatians 2:12.
8. Morris, Leon. *Galatians: Paul's Charter of Christian Freedom*. Downers Grove: InterVarsity, 1996. p.24. Morris is a good commentator overall, and he admits that Paul was not against Jewish believers keeping the Law. Yet his statement here too strongly criticizes the Law and also erroneously divides it into ritual and moral commandments.

9.   ibid. p.154. By contrast, John says, "For this is the love of God, that we keep his commandments. And his commandments are not burdensome" (1 John 5:3).

10. McKnight, Scott. *Galatians: NIV Application Commentary*. Grand Rapids: Zondervan, 1995. p.30. Jesus would be surprised to know that the era of the Law ended. He said, "Until heaven and earth pass away, not an iota, not a dot, will pass from the Law until all is accomplished" (Matt. 5:18).

11. Boice, James Montgomery. "Galatians," in *The Zondervan NIV Commentary on the New Testament*. Grand Rapids: Zondervan, 1994. p.726.

12. Stott, John. *The Message of Ephesians*. Downer's Grove: InterVarsity, 1979. p.101. Stott accepts the solution that when Jesus said the Law would not be abolished, he meant only the Laws considered moral, whereas he always intended to abolish the other Laws. This interpretation hardly fits Jesus' words: "until heaven and earth pass away, not an iota, not a dot, will pass from the Law" (Matt. 5:18). What would be the point of Jesus emphasizing even the smallest iota or tittle if he really meant that ? of the Law would be abolished?

13. Acts 21:20-26.

14. Acts 16:3.

15. 1 Corinthians 9:8-9.

16. Romans 10:3.

17. Even this idea, that the religious Jewish establishment interpreted Torah as a system of self-righteousness, does not mean what many think. First-century Jews did not exactly believe what is now termed as Pelagianism (we earn our standing before God by our righteousness). Rather, they understood the concept of forgiveness, but saw salvation as a more corporate affair. Israel needed to be saved from exile and the way to achieve this was to obey Torah. This was a system of self-righteousness, but it was not so individual as Pelagianism, the error Augustine, Martin Luther, and others read back into the writings of Paul.

18. Romans 7:4.

19. 1 Corinthians 9:20.

20. Galatians 3:13.

Chapter 4 Notes: Acts and Paul

1. Acts 21:30.
2. Mishnah Nazir 1:3.
3. Acts 18:18.
4. Normally a person would shave his hair on day one, be sprinkled with water on day three and seven, then offer two turtledoves on day eight, and restart the vow (Mishnah Nazir 7:2).
5. Hebrews 9:9, 10:4.
6. Verses such as Leviticus 15:31 and Numbers 35:34 show that the concern of the sacrificial system was to preserve the purity of the land so God can dwell there. With regard to the atonement language of Leviticus, as Jacob Milgrom (*Leviticus: Anchor Bible Series*) observes, the sacrifices atone for the tabernacle and its furniture directly but on behalf of (not directly) the offerer.
7. Ezekiel 40-48 describes a temple that has never been built along with a system of sacrifices, land allotment, and Messianic features that can only convincingly be interpreted as a yet-to-be-fulfilled prophecy of the days of Messiah. Those who try to allegorize these chapters of Ezekiel make a mockery of Biblical interpretation, opening to door to any wild allegorical rendering.
8. Acts 21:21.
9. Overheard in a sermon by Murray Tilles of Light of Messiah Ministries in Atlanta, Georgia. As I understand it, this statement originated with sermons used by the Jews For Jesus ministry based in San Francisco, California.
10. Some interpret it differently, but in the ensuing exposition I will seek to prove my point.
11. People often speak of converting to Judaism, not Jewishness, but this can be misleading. It is not so much a religion that is being converted to as a people with an allegiance to God. Jewishness is not a race or religion, but a peoplehood, which is a larger concept. Many in Israel had Gentile ancestry (Joseph's wife was Egyptian, Moses' first was a Midianite and his second a Cushite, and the list goes on). Israel was a people from whom the native-born could be cut off and into whom strangers could be adopted.
12. Acts 15:1.
13. Acts 15:5.
14. Acts 23:6.

15. Acts 6:7.
16. Acts 15:9.
17. Acts 15:14.
18. Such as Isaiah 2:2-4 and Zechariah 8:23.
19. Historically this happened with a few individuals such as Naaman the Leper (2 Kings 5 and Luke 4:26) and the widow of Zarephath (1 Kings 17 and Luke 4:27).
20. Acts 15:19.
21. Hegg, Tim. *The Letter Writer: Paul's Background and Torah Perspective*. Tacoma: First Fruits of Zion, 2002. p.275.
22. 2 Kings 5:18.
23. This is not to say that Gentiles are not joined to Israel in other ways, as Paul makes clear in Romans 11:16-24. Gentiles are wild olive branches grafted into a natural olive tree. As wild branches grafted in, Gentiles retain their identity as non-Jews while sharing in the spiritual blessings of Israel. The physical blessings of Israel (ownership of the land and restoration in the days of Messiah) still belong to physical Israel (though only those of faith will inherit the promise).
24. Such thinking is rooted in a very false idea of morality: that we can know what is moral based on conscience and reason. Rather, morality is defined by God. If God forbids something, though we do not understand why, it is immoral to dissent from God. Justice is right because God is just. It is false to say that God is just because justice is right.
25. Exodus 31:17.
26. Numbers 15:38.
27. Deuteronomy 16:16.
28. Leviticus 11 and Deuteronomy 14:21.
29. Deuteronomy 14:21 says that the meat can be sold to Gentiles and emphasizes that Israel may not eat it because they are a chosen people, separated from the nations.
30. Acts 15:21.
31. Marshall, I. Howard. *Acts: Tyndale New Testament Commentary*. Leicester: Inter-Varsity Press, 1980. p.254.
32. Resnik, Russ. "Is the Torah Only for Jews? The Relationship of Jew and Non-Jew in God's Covenant", umjc.org.
33. Acts 18:2 refers to Jews ejected from Rome by the Emperor Claudius. According to Seutonius (*Life of Claudius* 25:4), this

expulsion occurred because of rioting in the streets between Jews and Messianic Jews over the issue of Chrestus (Christ).

34. Acts 13:14, 14:1, etc.
35. Acts 16:13, 18:4.
36. Acts 20:16.
37. Acts 23:6.
38. Acts 21:21, 24.

Chapter 5 Notes: Paul Preaching to Jews and God-Fearers

1. Acts 13:13-14.
2. McRay, John. *Paul: His Life and Teaching*. Grand Rapids: Baker, 2003. p.122, n.72. McRay is an authority on archaeology behind the New Testament. He notes that in eastern Syria a church and a synagogue were found near to each other. Both were in homes enlarged and modified to accommodate larger crowds. Some towns did have actual synagogue buildings in the first century, and some have been found in Masada, Herodium, Gamla, and Delos (p.122, n.73).
3. Acts 13:16.
4. Acts 2:10; 6:5; 13:43.
5. Acts 10:2, 22; 13:16, 26, 43, 50; 16:14; 17:4, 17; 18:7.
6. John was well-known to Jews throughout the empire. Josephus recorded the death of John and noted that many Jews considered Herod Agrippa to have killed an innocent man.
7. Mark 15:21.
8. Paul used the word cross 10 times in his letters in such references as 1 Corinthians 1:17.
9. Leviticus 26:16.
10. Leviticus 26:17.
11. Deuteronomy 28:29.
12. Galatians 3:13.
13. Acts 13:39.
14. Romans 8:1-2.

Chapter 6 Notes: Beginning to Understand Galatians

1. Tertullian, *Against Marcion*, Book 5, Chapter 3.
2. Adam Clarke's Commentary on the Bible, Galatians 2:17.
3. Matthew 5:17.
4. Jamieson, Fausset, and Brown Commentary on the Bible, Galatians 2:18.

5. Leviticus 11-15 deal with the causes of and solutions to uncleanness.
6. Acts 11:2.
7. Acts 11:3.
8. Acts 15:14-15.
9. Galatians 2:12. The circumcision is a broad term for Jews and, I would argue, does not refer to the men from James, but to some other group of Jews.
10. Luke 6:15.
11. Bruce, F.F. *The Epistles to the Galatians: New International Greek Testament Commentary.* Grand Rapids: Eerdmans, 1982. p.130.
12. Galatians 1:14.

Chapter 7 Notes: Unraveling the Drama of Galatians
1. Galatians 1:6.
2. Galatians 1:7,9.
3. Jamieson, Fausset, and Brown Commentary on the Bible, Galatians
4. 1:7.
5. Adam Clarke's Commentary on the Bible, Galatians 1:7.
6. Nanos, Mark. *The Irony of Galatians.* Minneapolis: Fortress Press, 2002. p.259.
7. ibid. p.260.
8. ibid. p.258.
9. Acts 13:47 and many others.
10. Acts 15:17.
11. Galatians 5:16.

Chapter 8 Notes: Romans — Israel and the Gentiles
1. Romans 11:18.
2. Romans 1:16.
3. Romans 1:25.
4. Romans 2:17ff. Nomism refers to the idea that all the people of Israel are made right with God simply by belonging to the covenant people. This is very different from the common depiction of Jews as legalists, earning their standing with God by observing the Law. Legalism does enter into some streams of Judaism, but nomism is far more common.
5. See chapter 6 concerning Galatians. Nanos, Mark. The Irony of Galatians. Minneapolis: Fortress Press, 2002.

6. Nanos, Mark. The Mystery of Romans. Minneapolis: Fortress Press, 1996.

7. ibid, p.94.

8. ibid., p.89.

9. ibid., pp.98-99.

10. Romans 14:15.

11. Nanos, Romans. Pp.64-68.

12. Suetonius, *Life of Claudius*, 25:2, cited in Moo, Douglas. *The Epistle to the Romans: New International Commentary on the New Testament*. Grand Rapids: Eerdmans, 1996. p.4.

13. Nanos argues that we should not assume Priscilla and Aquila were disciples, but Witherington counters with arguments I find persuasive: (1) if they were not disciples one would think Paul would proselytize them and (2) it was Paul's practice to stay with disciples wherever he went. Witherington, Ben III, with Hyatt, Darlene. *Paul's Letter to the Romans: A Socio-Rhetorical Commentary*. Grand Rapids: Eerdmans, 2004.

14. Orosius, *Hist.* VII 6:15. Dio Cassius, 60.6.6. Nanos argues that Cassius is refuting Suetonius' claim about the expulsion. This may be true, but he at least confirms some action was taken against the Jews. Acts 18:2 seems decisive, for if Priscilla and Aquila were expelled, the action must have been fairly broad (even if the entire Jewish population was not expelled). Cf. Nanos, p.374. Witherington thinks the reference in Cassius is to a different event in 41 C.E. cf. Witherington, p.12.

15. Nanos argues against this entire scenario. Key to his argument is Acts 28:22, in which, he claims, the Jewish leaders express a lack of knowledge concerning the beliefs of the Jesus-followers. This would be devastating to the Jewish expulsion theory except Acts 28:22 does not indicate the Jewish leaders did not know the beliefs of the Jesus-followers. They wanted to hear out Paul, whom they had more reason to respect as a Pharisee and a Jewish leader of distinction . cf. Nanos, p.376.

16. MacMullen, Ramsay. *Paganism in the Roman Empire*. New Haven and London: Yale University Press, 1981. Cited in Nanos, p.66.

17. Nanos, p.66 and also footnote 82.

18. Romans 3:1-2.

19. Romans 7:12.

20. Romans 9:4-5, 10:1, 11:26.

21. There is similarity to Nanos's conclusion and Witherington's, although Witherington thinks Paul has turned away from Judaism and the Law. Nanos sees Romans as Paul writing to get the Roman disciples to be more respectful of the Jewish community. Witherington sees Paul as promoting Jewish disciples and Israel in their eyes with a view to end conflicts in the congregation.

22. John Calvin, *Commentaries on the Epistle of Paul the Apostle to the Romans*, trans. and ed. John Owen (Grand Rapids: Baker Book House, reprinted 1993), p. 437.

23. Moo, p.831.

24. Witherington, p.15.

Chapter 9 Notes: Ephesians 2 — One New Man

1. Ephesians 6:2-3.

2. Lincoln, Andrew T. Ephesians: *Word Biblical Commentary*. Dallas: Word, 1990. p.141.

3. Numbers 15:14.

4. Deuteronomy 7:3.

5. Deuteronomy 7:4.

6. John 18:28, the priests worried that entering Pilate's hall would defile them for the next day's Passover khagigah offering.

7. Mark 7:5, the issue discussed here is not types of meat as many assume but ritual handwashing. The Pharisees believed that uncleanness could be spread by various means, including contact with Gentiles who carried impurity, and contracted trough eating food touched by hands that had not been ritually purified.

8. Luke 16:8 is probably a reference to the Essenes (sons of light) who refused interaction with anyone other than tediously pure practitioners. Implied is rejection of Gentile contact.

9. Lincoln, p.141. He cites Josephus, Antiquities 15.11.5, Jewish War 5.5.2.

10. Barth, Markus. *Ephesians 1-3: The Anchor Bible*. Garden City: Doubleday. 1974. p.287.

11. ibid., pp.287-291.

12. ibid., p.288.

13. Romans 7:13.

14. Ephesians 3:6.

15. Ephesians 2:18.

Chapter 10 Notes: Paul's Kingdom Thought

1. A small and very incomplete list of passages about the restoration of Israel in the last days would have to include: Deuteronomy 30:1-10, Isaiah 2:1-4, Jeremiah 31:33, Ezekiel 11:16-20, 36:24-38, 37:1-14, Zechariah 10:6-10, 12:9-10, 14:1-17.
2. Deuteronomy 30:6.
3. Jeremiah 31:33.
4. Ezekiel 36:26-27.
5. I don't think Peter is disagreeing with this in 2 Peter 3:12 when he speaks of us waiting for and hastening the day of his coming. Our obedience does contribute to God's plan and thus speeds the kingdom's arrival. Nonetheless, it is God's timing not ours. Our part is only to obey and wait.
6. In the Acts 9 account, Jesus tells Ananias about Paul's ministry to Gentiles in vs.15, but no mention is made to Paul.
7. Acts 22:21.
8. Romans 4:5 would be just one example.
9. 2 Corinthians 3:18.
10. Ephesians 1:4.

Chapter 11 Notes: Paul's Thought in a Nutshell

1. Eoster was a Teutonic fertility goddess celebrated in the springtime. Her biblical name was Ashtarte and in the Middle East was known as Ishtar. Through Greek mythology we are familiar with her as Aphrodite or Venus.
2. 1 Corinthians 9:20.
3. Galatians 2:11-14.
4. Romans 11:18.
5. Romans 7:14.
6. Galatians 4:9.
7. Romans 7:16.
8. Matthew 5:17-19.
9. Galatians 3:13.
10. Romans 8:2.
11. Romans 8:1.
12. Galatians 3:24-25.
13. Romans 9:6-13.
14. 1 Corinthians 10:5.
15. Romans 11:2-3.

16. Romans 11:17-21.
17. Romans 11:18.
18. 1 Corinthians 10:12.
19. Romans 11:21.
20. Romans 11:28.
21. Romans 11:29.
22. Romans 11:26.
23. Along with Mark Nanos, I take this to be the real point of Romans 14.
24. Romans 14:15.
25. Romans 11:5.
26. Romans 11:28.
27. Romans 11:27.
28. Romans 10:14-19.
29. Acts 22:21.
30. Romans 4:1-12, Galatians 3:8-9.
31. Romans 4:10-11.
32. A paraphrase of Genesis 12:3.
33. Galatians 3:8.
34. Hosea 2:23.
35. Romans 9:25.
36. Acts 15:17.
37. Amos 9:12.
38. Ephesians 2:12-13.
39. Ephesians 2:14-16.
40. Exodus 31:13.
41. Romans 14:1-6.
42. Acts 15:1-21.
43. Galatians 4:10.
44. Romans 14:5-8 would seemingly apply to Gentiles as well as Jews.
45. Ephesians 6:1-3, 1 Timothy 5:17-19, for example.
46. As is all too common in modern churches, the Bible was read as a practical handbook for modern living. Verses were interpreted as self-help principles. Verses were not taken in the context of the unfolding revelation of God from beginning to end.
47. 2 Timothy 3:16.

Bibliography

Note: Resources highly recommended for further reading are in bold.

Barth, Markus. Ephesians 1-3: *The Anchor Bible.* **Garden City: Doubleday. 1974.**

Boice, James Montgomery. "Galatians," in *The Zondervan NIV Commentary on the New Testament.* Grand Rapids: Zondervan, 1994.

Bruce, F.F. *Paul: Apostle of the Heart Set Free.* Grand Rapids: Eerdmans, 1998 (original edition 1977).

Bruce, F.F. *The Epistles to the Galatians: New International Greek Testament Commentary.* **Grand Rapids: Eerdmans, 1982.**

John Calvin, *Commentaries on the Epistle of Paul the Apostle to the Romans*, trans. and ed. John Owen (Grand Rapids: Baker Book House, reprinted 1993).

Hegg, Tim. *The Letter Writer: Paul's Background and Torah Perspective.* **Tacoma: First Fruits of Zion, 2002.**

Lincoln, Andrew T. *Ephesians: Word Biblical Commentary.* Dallas: Word, 1990.

MacMullen, Ramsay. *Paganism in the Roman Empire.* New Haven and London: Yale University Press, 1981.

Maier, Paul L. *The New Complete Works of Josephus.* Grand Rapids: Kregel, 1999.

Marshall, I. Howard. *Acts: Tyndale New Testament Commentary.* Leicester: Inter-Varsity Press, 1980.

McKnight, Scott. *Galatians: NIV Application Commentary.* Grand Rapids: Zondervan, 1995.

McRay, John. *Paul: His Life and Teaching*. Grand Rapids: Baker, 2003.

Moo, Douglas. *The Epistle to the Romans: New International Commentary on the New Testament*. Grand Rapids: Eerdmans, 1996.

Morris, Leon. Galatians: *Paul's Charter of Christian Freedom*. Downers Grove: InterVarsity, 1996.

Nanos, Mark. *The Irony of Galatians*. Minneapolis: Fortress Press, 2002.

Nanos, Mark. *The Mystery of Romans*. Minneapolis: Fortress Press, 1996.

Roetzel, Calvin. "Paul in the Second Century," in *The Cambridge Companion to St. Paul*, ed. James D.G. Dunn. Cambridge: Cambridge University Press, 2003.

Stott, John. *The Message of Ephesians*. Downer's Grove: InterVarsity, 1979.

Witherington, Ben III, with Hyatt, Darlene. *Paul's Letter to the Romans: A Socio-Rhetorical Commentary*. Grand Rapids: Eerdmans, 2004.

Wright, N.T. *What St. Paul Really Said*. Grand Rapids: Eerdmans, 1997.

Mt. Olive Press
P.O. Box 659
Stone Mountain, GA 30086
mtolivepress.com

Mt. Olive
Press

Books about the Jewish background of faith in Jesus.

Coming in 2005...
Rabbi and Redeemer: A Messianic Jewish Perspective on John
By David Mishkin

Coming in 2006...
Jesus Didn't Read the New Testament: Renewing Love for the Hebrew Bible
By Derek Leman

Quick Order Form

You can order by mail or by internet. Mail-in payments must be by check or money order. Credit Card orders can be made on our website.

Mt. Olive Press

Mt. Olive Press
P.O. Box 659
Stone Mountain, GA 30086
www.mtolivepress.com

For single copies please send $17.95 ($14.95 plus $3.00 shipping and handling). For additional copies add $16.50. Books will ship within 5 business days of your order. You may return the book for a full refund if not satisfied.

Resellers, please contact Mt. Olive Press for a competitive discount schedule.

Ship Order to:

_____

Name

_____

Address

_____

Apt #

_____

City, State, Zip

_____

Copies